Praise for *Gwen Jorgensen*

"Gwen's story proves that any girl can have a gigantic dream. From everyday young athlete to aspiring Olympic champion, Gwen's story rings true and emanates inspiration."
–Alexi Pappas, 2016 Olympian and author of Bravey

....

"Sprinkled with advice from adult Gwen to her younger self, this inspirational story gives the reader an inside look at the journey from little swimmer earning a ribbon to a triathlete earning an Olympic gold medal."
–Barb Lindquist, 2004 Olympian, Triathlon

....

"I would have enjoyed reading this book as a young aspiring athlete. Gwen's story is relatable to many in that she came from humble beginnings and slowly chipped away at her big goal. Her never give up attitude and dedication to reaching her goal to be an Olympian will be inspiring to all."
–Flora Duffy, 2020 Olympic gold medalist, Triathlon

....

"This may have been written for young adults, but anyone of any age will finish the book deeply inspired to pursue their goals—big or small—with passion and heart."
–Liza Wiemer, award-winning author of *The Assignment*

....

"This book encapsulates Gwen's remarkable journey to winning Olympic gold in triathlon. There are so many wonderful lessons and there is so much to be gleaned in Gwen Jorgensen: *USA's First Olympic Gold Medal Triathlete*."
–Taylor Knibb, 2020 Olympic medalist, Triathlon

....

"It's a special experience to be able to read in detail the background of an Olympic gold medalist, not just about her triumphs but also the challenges, setbacks, and uncertainties along the way."
–Katie Zaferes, 2016 Olympian and two-time 2020 Olympic medalist, Triathlon

Gwen Jorgensen | Elizabeth Jorgensen | Nancy Jorgensen

Gwen Jorgensen

USA's First Olympic Gold Medal Triathlete

Meyer & Meyer Sport

British Library of Cataloguing in Publication Data
A catalogue record for this book is available from the British Library
Gwen Jorgensen
Maidenhead: Meyer & Meyer Sport (UK) Ltd., 2023

ISBN: 978-1-78255-247-5

© 2023 by Meyer & Meyer Sport (UK) Ltd.
Aachen, Auckland, Beirut, Cairo, Cape Town, Dubai, Hägendorf, Hong Kong, Indianapolis, Maidenhead,
Manila, New Delhi, Singapore, Sydney, Tehran, Vienna
Member of the World Sport Publishers' Association (WSPA), www.w-s-p-a.org

Printed by Integrated Books International
Printed in the United States of America

ISBN: 978-1-78255-247-5
E-Mail: info@m-m-sports.com
www.thesportspublisher.com

Contents

Foreword

This is the story of Gwen Jorgensen—an accountant turned "Queen of Triathlon". Her rise to the top was swift. She won elite, professional races and qualified for the London Olympics within two years of taking up the sport. By 2015, she was a back-to-back world champion, and in 2016, in Rio de Janeiro, she became the first American to ever win Olympic Gold in a sport invented in California.

But don't be confused. This is not a story of greatness simply bestowed at birth.

When seen through the lens of those six years, you might think that Gwen was a natural and that winning Olympic gold was her destiny. However, this family heirloom of a book, bursting with optimism and written with love by Gwen's mother and sister, tells a deeper tale.

Sure, Gwen dreamed of the Olympics from the time she was a little girl, but she always considered herself a swimmer. The pool is where she found her strength and individuality, met her best friend, and fell in love with competing. She was good. Really good. She won races all over town and was one of the best on her high school swim team, but she wasn't fast enough to earn a scholarship to a top swim program, and by the time she was 18, it was clear that making the Olympic swim team was never going to happen.

Fortunately, Gwen Jorgensen wasn't just a good swimmer. She was a talented runner. Twice she was recruited by track coaches, once in high school and again in college. Although she didn't love running as much as swimming, she took their advice and pivoted. She was so good on the collegiate track that by the time she graduated she had an opportunity to pursue a professional career. Instead, she played it safe and took a job with a big accounting firm. It was the sensible thing to do. Most professional runners don't make a very good living. They do it for the love. At 22 years old, that wasn't enough for Gwen, and it seemed that her Olympic dreams were dead.

When coaches with the US Triathlon team approached her about getting into their sport with an eye on the London Olympics, her competitive fire reignited like a torch, and her future began to crystalize. They came to her because of her strong swim and run background, but when it came to the bike, she couldn't have been less experienced. She hardly even knew how to shift gears!

The point is, talent alone did not lift Gwen Jorgensen to the top of the triathlon universe, and that's what makes her story and this book so potent. She succeeded by falling in love with the process of controlling the controllables—all the little details that make up an athlete's life—and staying committed to getting a little bit better every single day.

But how do you do that when things seem to be going wrong? When injury, mishap, or malfunction surfaces and makes it impossible to achieve your immediate goals? How do you keep going when everything you see and hear makes you doubt yourself and question your future? Gwen did it by staying positive even in the face of negativity. "There is power in what you tell yourself," the Jorgensens write. She trained herself to look forward, not back. She concentrated only on what was to come.

Gwen cultivated mental and physical toughness—it takes a lot of grit and pain tolerance to excel in endurance sports—and lived life with intention. She didn't simply accept things as they were. She made her own way. She walked on to her college swim team. She sought out the coaching she needed to become a world champion, even when that meant moving to a different continent and far away from family and friends. She adopted dozens of small life hacks that helped her stay on course. You will find them within the main story, but also as additional tips slotted between chapters, alongside photographs, and the occasional recipe.

This book is packed with powerful life lessons whether or not you are an athlete. We all have dreams and will encounter obstacles as we learn and grow, but if you are a young woman who loves to compete in athletics, it will read like a road map. It will encourage you to never give up on your dream, teach you to accept intelligent guidance, embrace gratitude, and show you the power that comes from focusing on each day, each race or game, as another opportunity to be better.

The potential to do great things—whatever those things may be—resides deep within all of us. It lies dormant, beckoning to be harnessed. May this book help unlock your version of Gwen—and set you on a path to achieve your most outlandish dreams.

–Rich Roll, author of *Finding Ultra*

A Letter from Gwen

Dear Reader,

In elementary school, I wanted to be an Olympic swimmer. I imagined wearing the USA red, white and blue, my name first on the scoreboard. I dreamed of hearing the "Star-Spangled Banner" while I stood at the top of the awards podium.

Swimming dominated my life, from practices and competition to nutrition and recovery. Some of my races scored wins, but many did not. I believed if I worked harder and spent more time in the pool, I would get to the Olympics.

While my friends' times qualified them for regional meets, girls from other cities beat me at State and I never qualified for Junior Nationals or the Olympic trials. I felt like I did something wrong. That I should have been better.

So, you might be surprised to know that I am a two-time World Champion and at age 30, I became an Olympic champion. You might be more surprised to know that I'm the first USA athlete, man or woman, to win an Olympic gold medal in triathlon!

This is my story. After you read it, I hope you work to make your dream come true. Whether that is to be a famous artist or to revolutionize the gaming industry or cure a disease or even to be an Olympian, I hope you are inspired to try, to fail, to thank those who help you, and to find success.

Tell me about your goals. Post them on my social media pages, and I'll do my best to give you encouragement, a "like" or a thumbs up.

Love,
Gwen

CHAPTER 1

Rio 2016: Seven Days Before the Olympic Triathlon

"There is just so much to being the best that you can be."

—Gwen Jorgensen

Gwen Jorgensen planned to win the 2016 Olympic triathlon. She said it in interviews, she posted it on Instagram, she wrote it in her journal. In seven days, she would have her opportunity.

Gwen had been training in Spain where the sun was always hot. On this day, a fan whirred, blowing an arid breeze through her window. Sweat poured down her back. In 24 hours, she and her husband Patrick would be on a plane to Rio de Janeiro, Brazil, where she would face the ultimate test in strength, endurance and training.

There was so much to remember, yet Gwen felt calm. Five suitcases gaped open, waiting to be packed. She added wetsuits, goggles and swim caps. Sports bras, running shorts, training shoes. One bag held her bike with two sets of wheels, a tire pump, inner tubes and helmets. When filled, each would weigh 50 pounds.

"Patrick," she said, "do we have everything for the bikes?" Patrick had been a professional cyclist and now helped maintain her equipment. He loaded a spoked wheel into the largest bag, wrestling it next to a bike frame. "And did you remember the toolkit?"

"I'm working from our list," he said as he added a bike pump and extra tire. "I think we have it all. I've got both bikes and your training wheels packed. I don't see your helmet, though."

Gwen looked over his shoulder at the list and pointed. "You're good. I checked it off already. Did you reserve the team van for tomorrow morning?"

"Yup. One of the coaches will drive us."

In her six years as a professional athlete, racing in North America, South America, Europe, Africa, Asia and Australia, Gwen learned to make lists. It helped her control what she could, and it gave her peace of mind. Plus, it was the only way she remembered everything. She felt confident about her packing for Brazil and her race at the Olympics.

The next day, she would travel in the van 90 minutes north to the Bilbao, Spain, airport. Her final destination: the Rio 2016 Olympic Games. At stake was her Olympic dream and the first USA Olympic gold medal in triathlon.

Gwen's Packing Tips

- Make a list. Use an app or phone notes and reuse lists, adding or subtracting items as needed.
- Be specific. For example: 4 tights, 3 shorts, 3 shirts.
- Remember things that cannot be purchased—cash, credit cards, passport.
- For big trips, allow extra time to pack.
- While packing, evaluate belongings to donate or give away.

CHAPTER 2

1994 *Third Grade*

At Heyer Elementary School in Waukesha, Wisconsin, Gwen's teacher handed out a flyer. Sending papers down the rows, she said, "For all you swimmers, there is a special event next weekend. It's free and very popular. Our local Optimist Club runs a one-day swim meet. It's a day of learning. If you're interested, show your parents and have them read the directions for how to register."

The rest of the day, Gwen couldn't get swimming out of her head. She thought about summer days with her cousins at Grandma's pool. She imagined playing Marco Polo. She remembered how it felt to jump from a scorching diving board into cool water. She recalled racing her dad and her sister, arms and feet splashing, and wondered if she could win a real race.

After school that day, she ran in the door, shouting, "Mom, Mom," the swim meet permission slip in hand. "You have to sign this! Please! I need to swim in this meet."

"Hmm," her mom said, looking at the form. "I think the neighbors did this last year."

"Please, Mom?"

"Dad and I can talk about it."

"Dad will say yes. Please!" Gwen needed to do this. On television, she saw swimmers sail from regulation diving blocks into an Olympic-sized pool with colored lane markers. She knew she could do it, too.

"I'll check the schedule," her mom said. "As long as we're free, I don't see why not."

**

At the one-day event, Gwen heard about starting blocks, race officials, heats and scoreboards. For a warm-up lap, she used the freestyle stroke taught in swim lessons. She breathed side to side. She kicked and pulled. Then, she lined up on the pool deck for her first race.

Standing on top of the starting block, she felt nervous about diving headfirst, but girls on her left and right didn't look scared. They look determined. Gwen mimicked their actions, adjusting her goggles, and then focused on the official.

At the signal, Gwen crouched and grabbed the edge of the block. When the gun sounded, she dove in, came up for air and stroked arm over arm. She loved the sensation of moving fast, air rushing through her lips, bubbling up in her lane.

She reached the end of the pool, gulping oxygen as her chest rose and fell. Chlorine stung her nose, all the way to her throat. She spat water and looked around. A few had finished, but others were still swimming. Her body tingled with the rush of being one of the fastest.

Gwen hoisted herself to the deck and a woman gave her a ribbon. Gwen tucked it in her towel and pressed it close. As she waited for her next race, she uncovered her prize. She was proud of her first ribbon and wondered how much faster she could go.

In the car on the way home, Gwen said, "Can I join the swim team?" She wanted to practice. She wanted a coach to teach her. She wanted to swim faster.

Her parents exchanged a look, and then Dad said, "We know you're excited, but Mom and I need to look at the cost and see if we can make the schedule work."

"Please?"

"Dad and I have heard good things about Waukesha Express, but are you sure you want to swim twice a week? If we sign you up, you can't quit."

Gwen wouldn't quit. She wanted to swim every day. She hoped there would be meets every weekend, too. "I know, Mom. I'm positive. Can I?"

Swimming would be her activity, a sport no one else in the family did. Not Mom, not Dad and not her sister Elizabeth. Not even her cousins. It would be hers alone, a place to practice and excel.

***

Gwen's parents agreed to one 12-week session, so every Tuesday and Thursday, her dad drove her to Waukesha South High School. Coach Blaine Carlson showed Gwen the proper way to grip a paddle board for kick sets and how to use a buoy on pull sets. Each week, she swam laps, practiced dives and prepared for competition.

She made friends with Allison, Tristine and Katie Mae. They created games to keep track of laps. They talked between sets and shared secrets in the locker room. The four girls planned to swim in high school and college and vowed to work hard and improve their speed. They agreed to eat healthy foods, filling their plates with broccoli, carrots and apples. A few times, they ate ice cream and then Gwen said, "It's made from milk, so it has a lot of calcium."

At practice, Gwen and her friends learned the competitive strokes: freestyle, butterfly, backstroke and breaststroke. Each one found her own strongest strokes: Gwen freestyle; Allison butterfly; Tristine butterfly and breaststroke; Katie Mae butterfly and backstroke.

***

On the day of her first Waukesha Express swim meet, Gwen's dad dropped her off at the pool. The moon shone full, the morning sky still dark. When she stepped into the entryway, her footsteps echoed in the empty space. Was she the first swimmer to arrive? In the locker room, she changed into her swimsuit and shivered from the cold air and freezing floor. But on the pool deck, steam rose. Gwen breathed the chlorine scent. She loved it. It reminded her of her friends and the smooth, clean feel of the water

Coach Blaine put Gwen, Allison, Tristine and Katie Mae in a relay. At their turn, they huddled behind the starting block. Katie Mae hopped in the water for backstroke. The whistle blew and she pushed off. Gwen, Allison and Tristine cheered even though so many kids were shouting, Katie Mae probably couldn't hear them. Tristine climbed up the starting block, bent forward, and when Katie Mae tagged the wall, Tristine launched into the water. Gwen yelled as loud as she could for Tristine and then for Allison. Nerves prickled under Gwen's skin because she was the anchor. It was up to her to win.

Gwen dove in with a tiny lead over the other teams. She plunged her head under the water and breathed only when necessary. A girl in the next lane caught up and that's when Gwen kick, kick, kicked! She moved ahead an inch and hoped to hold her off. Gwen stretched her arms and after one last stroke,

Grandma and Grandpa's pool

glided to the pool edge and slapped the gutter. When she looked up, Allison, Tristine and Katie Mae were jumping and cheering. They pointed to the scoreboard. Gwen turned to look. Her team held the number one spot with the fastest time. They won!

In the car on the way home, Dad said, "Good job on your personal best."

Gwen looked up at him. "I always swim faster in relays."

"Why is that?"

"Because I can't let my friends down. I have to be fast so they can win."

Allison, Katie Mae, Gwen

How Gwen Learned to Use a Starting Block

A starting block is a raised platform at one end of a pool lane. It is usually within 29 ½ inches from the water. For safety, the pool must be deep enough to prevent injury when a person dives. USA Swimming recommends a pool has "a minimum pool-depth of four feet at the shallow end and seven feet at the starting block end."

At practices, Gwen and her friends lined up behind the starting block. At their turn, they mounted the block, waited for the coach's whistle and dove in. When they climbed out of the pool, they listened to feedback from the coach and got back in line again.

CHAPTER 3

1995 Fourth Grade

During a Sunday dinner in June, Mom and Dad told Elizabeth and Gwen about a one-week vacation. Elizabeth acted excited, but Gwen was horrified. "No way." She slapped her hand on the table for extra emphasis. "I can't miss two swim practices and a meet."

She needed all the pool time she could get. Katie Mae, Allison and Tristine swam faster every week, but Gwen's times improved more slowly. If she just worked harder, she could catch up.

"Gwen, calm down," her mom said. "We'll go during your break between sessions. And we'll schedule water activities on the trip, like whitewater rafting."

Elizabeth said, "What's that?"

"It's like being in a canoe," Dad said. "But with rough water. We'll paddle, but mostly ride the current."

Gwen said, "I guess that sounds fun. But I better not miss any days in the pool." Coach Blaine said other sports improved coordination and speed. So, maybe rafting would better her race times.

In a few weeks, Dad drove them to a rural bait shop. When they entered, a screen door slapped behind them. The shop smelled musty, like worms. Flies buzzed around Gwen's head.

The owner of the rafting company talked to Mom and Dad about helmets and safety and made them read waivers. He pushed a paper and pen toward them. Mom asked lots of questions. "But, is it safe?" she said.

"There's always a risk—nature is unpredictable."

Mom looked at Dad. "Maybe we should do something else today?"

"No," Gwen said, her eyes pleading. "It'll be fun." Would Mom have them come all this way and not let them ride the river? Gwen imagined an adventure, a little wild, even more thrilling because it was on water. She wasn't afraid, even though Elizabeth told her it would be scary.

The group in front took off for the river.

Gwen was thankful when Dad signed the form.

"Let's go get our raft," he said.

At the river, the guide passed out helmets and life jackets. They smelled like a boys' locker room. Dozens of rafts lined the shore. The guide handed out paddles. "Each raft holds one group," he said. "Pick one. Kids, hang on to the ropes and stay close to your parents."

Gwen tugged the buckle of her orange life vest. She sat next to Dad, hoping he would let her paddle.

Dad pushed off. The first moments were calm, but suddenly, the raft tugged and jerked. Waves rocked and lifted it into the air. All around, water rose and pushed them faster. Elizabeth slid to the corner and cried. Mom took loud, deep breaths. Gwen leaned over the side and trailed her fingers through the cool, murky water. She slapped the waves. "Dad, this is so fun."

"Gwen, stop leaning over," Mom said. "Hold on to the side!"

"I'm fine, Mom," Gwen said. But Elizabeth looked scared. She crouched on the bottom, holding the straps so tight, her knuckles were white. What was up with her? This was a blast!

For two hours, they crashed down waterfalls, bumped over boulders and bounced on waves. When the waters calmed, they got stuck on a rock. Gwen asked Dad if she could paddle, but Mom shook her head. They shoved off and the ride started over, gliding and rushing like a rollercoaster.

At the end of the trip, Gwen's feet rested in a few inches of river water. She wrung out her hair and pictured them rafting again—this time, with her paddling. She bet it would improve her swim stroke. "Can we do it again tomorrow?" she asked.

Mom said, "I think we're all better off in the calm waters of a swimming pool."

Gwen frowned, but secretly looked forward to a few laps at the hotel.

Dad, Elizabeth and Gwen pretending to be exhausted after the whitewater raft trip

CHAPTER 4

1996 Fifth Grade

At school today, Gwen would participate in the big one-mile run. Last night, Gwen dreamed she came in first, ahead of all her classmates. She'd won!

For weeks, she prepared for The Presidential Physical Fitness Test. Now, she stood between the four-square and the jungle gym. The teacher explained the course. "When I blow the whistle, run four laps around the school." Some kids pushed to the front, whispering they wanted to win. Others hung at the back like they didn't want to run at all. The teacher said, "I'll time you on the stopwatch and you count your laps."

Gwen counted a lot of laps in swimming. Easy.

The teacher had set orange cones to mark the turns. She raised her arm. "Ready, set...GO!"

Gwen took off, pumping her arms, sprinting to the front. The air felt sticky. Sun reflected off the pavement. Soon, she and a few others led. They turned left at the first cone and disappeared around the school. After three more turns, Gwen passed the teacher and started lap two.

I'm not tired, she thought, and increased her speed. She and her group disappeared around the building and passed the teacher for lap three. All around her, kids breathed, loud and heavy.

Gwen's legs hurt and sweat trickled down her back, but she pushed to stay with the fastest runners. Rounding a corner, she spied a group she already lapped. One girl started to walk. A boy stopped and put his hands on his knees. Gwen's group split left and right to go around them. Gwen ran so fast, the wind blew her hair back.

By the end of the fourth lap, Gwen led all the girls and many of the boys. Not surprising. At swim practice, she ran as a warm-up and got faster each day.

When she crossed the finish line, she wanted to pump her fist in the air but didn't. If Gwen made top 15 percent in her grade, she would earn the award.

Gwen's group lined up to hear their times. The teacher said, "Gwen, why did you stop? You have another lap."

What!?! "Why? I just ran a mile."

"You couldn't have finished that fast. Run another."

Gwen didn't know what to do. She tried to think of a response, but the teacher's eyes narrowed. Why didn't the teacher believe her? Gwen's face burned and she blinked away tears. She stood there, stunned, unsure how to respond.

Gwen didn't want anyone to see her cry, so she joined the lapped group and ran. She felt angry, but concentrated on not crying.

After another lap, Gwen no longer finished first among the girls. She wouldn't be in the top 15 percent. There would be no Presidential Physical Fitness Award.

All afternoon, through math and art, she thought about the race. The minute she got home, she told her mom, "I'm so mad. I should have won. I'm the fastest."

Mom handed her an apple. "Your teacher doesn't know you can run that fast. She made a mistake."

21

Gwen bit and chewed, making extra noise. Anger boiled inside. Teachers shouldn't make mistakes. And they should believe their students. Especially her. She would never lie or cheat to win. She thought her teachers knew that.

Later that evening, on the drive to swim practice, Gwen tried to make Dad understand. "It's not fair!"

He turned on the radio. "Hey! 'Eye of the Tiger.' Your favorite song. That should make you feel better. And let's get ice cream after practice."

Gwen loved how Dad always wanted to help, but today, his ideas didn't work.

At the pool, she didn't tell Allison, Katie Mae and Tristine about the mile run. She wanted it to be far away.

Coach Blaine explained the workout. Gwen dove in and started the laps. At the first stroke, the world went quiet. Under the water, no one talked. No one accused her of making a mistake. No one tried to make her feel better. She found a rhythm in the strokes, and soon, the mile run didn't matter so much.

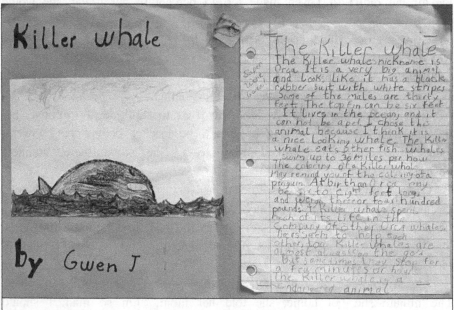

Gwen's water-related schoolwork

CHAPTER 5

1997 Sixth Grade

At home in the family room, Gwen flopped down next to Elizabeth. "This is the worst," she said. In physical education, tumbling felt awkward, she couldn't do a cartwheel, and her assignment was a gymnastics floor routine. "You have to help me."

At school, the gym teacher had said, "Practice until it's memorized. Include balance, somersaults, strength and flexibility."

Gwen choreographed a floor exercise and performed it over and over for Elizabeth, Mom and Dad. She wanted to do her best and she really wanted an A. Plus, Coach Blaine said better flexibility would improve her dives and strokes.

Gwen included all the elements, but every time she tried the somersault, she failed to tuck her head. Her body tipped sideways.

Elizabeth critiqued from a beanbag chair, directing Gwen where to place her hands and when to push forward. "The somersault needs work, but the rest looks great," she said, "so you should get an A."

Gwen hesitated to believe that, so she practiced more. Maybe repetition would help.

On test day, Gwen performed for the teacher and, as usual, bungled the somersault. She tried to not be angry or frustrated with herself. She noticed other kids biffed moves too.

At the end of class, the teacher handed out grades. Gwen flipped to the back page right away. C! She got a C! She stuffed the paper in her pocket. There's no way she deserved a C. That's average. Her routine was not average. The teacher didn't understand how much she practiced. She did everything right except one move.

At home, Gwen threw down her bag. "Stupid somersault. Just because it wasn't perfect doesn't mean I deserve a C."

"You can't always get an A," her mom said. "Don't let it bother you."

Gwen slammed her bedroom door, picked up her pillow and punched it. What could she have done differently? Practiced more? Asked someone on the swim team for a trick?

That night, as she helped her mom pack lunches, Gwen barely said a word. Mom put an arm around her and said, "You'll have plenty of chances to improve in phy ed. You don't have to be perfect every time."

Gwen nodded, fighting frustration, angry that her body wouldn't do what she wanted.

***

The next morning at breakfast, Mom said, "Summer vacation starts in a few weeks. I signed you both up for track camp." Elizabeth loved track, so Mom and Dad decided both girls would go. Gwen preferred one more swim session but didn't argue because Coach Blaine said running would improve endurance.

Track camp was at Waukesha West High School. Coach Ramsey supplied sports drinks and an agenda each day. Gwen liked time outdoors and that some girls from her swim team were there.

Coach Ramsey started practice by organizing runners into groups. "Time for drills," he said. "We'll do high knees and butt-kicks, but first let's start with backward runs." He demonstrated the starting position and shouted. "Go slow on the backward runs."

Gwen listened closely and paid attention. From swimming, she understood the importance of form, where she kept her elbows high and kicked on every stroke.

"Get your knees up and drive your arms parallel to the ground. This is not about speed. Take it easy. Don't hurt yourself."

Elizabeth's row of older kids went first.

Time for Gwen's group. She turned around, facing backward. Coach Ramsey blew the whistle and she took off, concentrating on placement—feet, knees, arms. This was easy. She could go faster for sure. She built up speed, swung her arms and soon led her group. But then she tripped. She tried to regain balance, but her body tilted ahead of her legs. She extended an arm and fell, fell, fell. It seemed like a long time in the air, tumbling to the hot rubber track.

Pain stabbed, sharp and stinging. Gwen tried to shake it away, but that made it worse. She looked down. Just above her wrist, one bone stuck up and one pointed down.

Coach Ramsey knelt next to her. "Gwen, stay put. Don't move," he said. "I'm putting my clipboard under your arm. It'll keep things in place. Rest here. I'm going to call your mom."

Gwen laid still, wishing this were a nightmare.

It felt like a long time before Mom arrived. "Oh, honey. How bad does it hurt?" She kissed Gwen's forehead.

"I can't move my arm." It was the worst pain Gwen ever felt, but she didn't want to scare her mom. She also didn't want anyone to see her cry. This will ruin swimming, she thought, biting her lip so tears didn't fall.

An assistant coach held her arm and the clipboard supporting it. "Let's get you in your mom's car. The hospital is close."

At the hospital, Mom got a wheelchair and pushed her to the emergency department where everything smelled like bleach. Air-conditioning blew through Gwen's damp t-shirt, making her shiver. Finally, a nurse called her name and took her to a room where a doctor examined her arm.

After X-rays and more waiting, the surgeon said, "You need an operation. Then we'll put a cast on your arm."

Panic hit. "Can I have one of those casts I can swim in?"

He shook his head. "I'm sorry, but it's not that kind of break."

Each time a nurse came into her room, Gwen begged for a water cast. Each time, they said, "You can't get your cast wet."

Gwen couldn't believe Mom made her do track. If she were swimming, this never would have happened. Now, everyone on the swim team would improve and leave her behind.

After midnight, the surgeon finished the procedure, wrapped her arm in heavy plaster, then a bandage and a sling. Gwen slept in a hospital bed and returned home the next day.

When Katie Mae heard about Gwen's broken arm, she called. "Oh, no. Gwen, you're my best lane buddy. And what if I forget my towel? You won't be there to share." Like always, she talked super-fast into the phone. It made Gwen smile even though she didn't feel like smiling. "But don't worry. You'll be back soon. I know it."

Katie Mae called after every swim practice to describe the workout. One day, she said, "Coach Blaine wants me in the Gold group."

Gwen's cast felt like concrete, weighing her down. "I knew everyone would move ahead without me."

"Don't worry. I told him no. I won't go unless you do. We always move together."

Gwen felt a little better but also guilty. What would happen to Katie Mae's times? Would they both be worse when Gwen returned? "It's okay, Katie. You should move up."

"Nope. Your cast will be off soon and then we'll swim in the same lane again. I'll let you draft behind me if you get tired. We'll move to Gold together."

Flopping back on her pillows, Gwen flipped through a book about Olympians. She imagined swimming with Katie Mae at the Olympic trials. She glanced at her cast, filled with messages and signatures from friends at school. She hated that cast. She just wanted to get back to the pool as fast as she could.

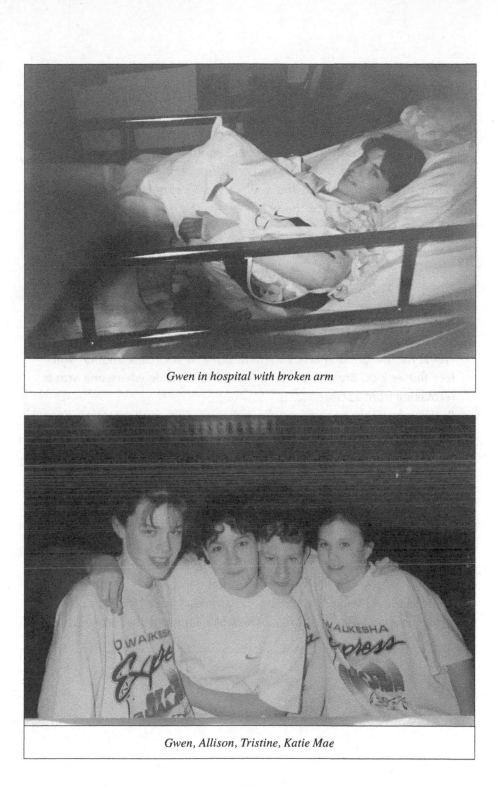

Gwen in hospital with broken arm

Gwen, Allison, Tristine, Katie Mae

Gwen Drafted at Swim Practice

Swimming behind another athlete saves energy, perhaps up to 30 percent. The best place to draft is directly behind another swimmer's feet.

Gwen and three or four swimmers alternated drafting in the pool. When the group reached the wall, a new swimmer took the lead. Alternating allowed all of the swimmers to share the work and receive the benefit of drafting.

Gwen Learned Swim Events

Freestyle: Lie on stomach. Alternate arms in a circular motion while feet flutter kick. Breathe by turning head to the side where one arm is recovering from a stroke.

Backstroke: Float on back and alternate arms in a circular motion. Keep feet under the water and flutter kick. Look straight up and keep face out of the water.

Breaststroke: Lie on stomach. Move arms at the same time, underwater in front of the body, in a half-circle. When arms reach the side, head comes out of the water for a breath. Coordinate arms with frog-kick legs.

Butterfly: Lie on stomach. Bring both arms over the head and push them into the water. As arms push into the water, push head and shoulders above the water. With legs, perform a dolphin kick, keeping legs straight and together, moving in a wave-like motion.

IM (Individual Medley): In this event, swimmers use all four competitive strokes in a set order—butterfly, backstroke, breaststroke and freestyle.

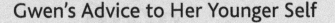

Gwen's Advice to Her Younger Self

Dear Elementary School Gwen,

Watching Katie Mae, Allison and Tristine makes you wonder what's wrong, why they're improving and you're not. You question yourself when you shower in the morning, while you eat breakfast and lunch, and when you're at swim practice. You doubt yourself and question your worth. But, Gwen, each person is different and that's okay. Each person has success at a different time.

Enjoy swimming. Enjoy your teammates. Enjoy meets and traveling with your family. Don't compare yourself to anyone else. Don't envy others' strengths. You have your own gifts. Write them down. Look at them. Celebrate them.

Gwen, I know you want immediate success and to be the best right now. But that's not how any of this works—not life, not school, not friends, not career. Someday, you will have an impact. You will have a voice. You will give back and make a difference. You will win the biggest meet of all.

Be patient and work hard. Enjoy your family, your team and your coaches. I know you're doubtful. But you have time. Don't focus on achievements, just love swimming and being around your favorite people.

Sincerely,
Adult Gwen

CHAPTER 6

Rio 2016: Six Days Before the Olympic Triathlon

"Be totally focused, go #allin."
—Gwen Jorgensen

Early on the morning of August 14, 2016, Gwen and Patrick shoved their bags into the team van's cargo space. Darkness lingered, only a few apartment windows lit, the parking lot deserted except for them and one coach. Gwen's legs felt stiff, and she longed for a quick shakeout run. But there was only time for a few calf stretches on the curb. She rolled her head and heard the familiar cracking sound.

Gwen's coach hopped in the driver's seat. "Got everything?" He had agreed to drop them at the Bilbao, Spain, airport.

"All set," she said. Although dreading the long flight to Rio de Janeiro, Brazil, excitement coursed through her. Finally, after four years of preparation, she was on her way to the Rio 2016 Olympic Games.

Gwen had been training in Vitoria-Gasteiz, Spain, with Coach Jamie Turner and the Wollongong Wizards—an international group of triathletes. Every day, they swam, biked and ran as both competitors and friends. When Sarah-Anne Brault from Canada ran fast, Gwen congratulated her and then tried to outrun her. When Barbara Riveros from Chile improved in the water, Gwen said, "Good job," and then worked to outswim her. Eight of the Wizards, including Gwen, qualified for the 2016 Olympic race. Her teammates represented Chile, Hungary, Canada and Australia. Gwen was the only Wizard racing for USA and she planned to win gold for her country.

On the ride to the airport, Patrick said, "I got an email from the airline, Gwen." He grinned. "You're gonna be happy."

"Did I get a good seat?" Gwen had requested first class, where she could put up her feet, sleep in a reclined chair and eat a better meal. Recovery and care for her body were as important as training.

"Yup. Now your legs won't be cramped for sixteen hours."

"Where will you be?"

"Seven rows behind you."

They paid the higher price for Gwen, but Patrick would sit in economy. Gwen was thankful Patrick didn't mind. He did so much—shopping, cooking, emails and now sacrificing his own comfort—so she could perform at her best.

"Enjoy it and get some rest," he said. "I'll come visit once in a while."

At airport ticketing, they piled their bags on the sidewalk. The area swarmed with travelers. When a stream of people came by, Gwen eyed her own bags so nothing disappeared.

"Gwen, stay here," Patrick said, "and I'll grab a cart."

Patrick retrieved a dolly, loaded their gear and pushed. Gwen slung a backpack over her shoulders and rested one hand on the tower of bags so it wouldn't topple. They joined the line at the ticket counter, waiting and waiting to check in. Gwen snapped a picture of their bags—a great Facebook shot.

Finally, they reached the front of the line. "Miss, those bags are too big for standard check-in. Please step to the special inspection area." Gwen and Patrick's luggage was frequently checked because of its size.

At the oversize luggage desk, the inspector said, "What's in all these?"

"Bikes, wheels, shoes, helmets. All athletic gear," Patrick said.

They waited for the inspector to look in containers, search equipment, poke in pockets.

"Good thing we got here early," Gwen said.

How to Fly with Gwen

Gwen's bags bound for Rio

Jet lag is a temporary sleep disorder that disrupts a person's internal clock. It can cause fatigue or insomnia when a person flies across time zones.

When Gwen traveled internationally, she felt these effects. She knew her body could adjust to one or two time zones per day, so she arrived in Rio several days before her race. Patrick followed her example and adjusted partially to the new time before leaving; they drank plenty of water; moved around on the plane; and adapted to the local schedule as soon as possible.

How Gwen Prepared for Rio de Janeiro Weather

Triathletes train in warm weather near an ocean or lake since the competitive swim is staged in open water. From January through April, Gwen and the Wollongong Wizards trained in Australia's summer. When the seasons changed, they chased summer to Spain and worked there during May, June, July and August.

Spain's hot weather allowed Gwen to prepare for Rio de Janeiro's winter: August in Brazil has an average high of 78°.

"We have plenty of time." Patrick put his arm around Gwen's shoulders. "Are you nervous?"

"Not really."

The inspector finished, nodded approval and charged them a few hundred dollars for the extra baggage.

Soon, they would be in the air, on their way to Brazil. For the biggest race of Gwen's life.

CHAPTER 7

2000 Ninth Grade

On the first day of high school swim practice, Coach Blaine said, "I want everyone to keep a journal." He stood on the pool deck, pacing in front of the bleachers where the team sat in swimsuits, towels around their shoulders. "Record each workout. Log how you feel. Describe your hopes and dreams. Make goals." He held up a spiral notebook. "It doesn't have to be fancy. Just a place to write."

Twice a day, just like Coach Blaine instructed, Gwen wrote in her journal.

***

About a month into swim season, Gwen exited the pool after morning workout, breathless from the last set. Chlorine hung in the air, sharp and familiar. She plopped on a pool-deck bench and pulled out her notebook. On the first page, she wrote in capital letters: GOALS. Underneath: Win a state championship. Go to Senior National Meet. Swim at Division I college. Qualify for Olympics. She added today's workout and made a plan for tomorrow: pack extra after-school snacks.

When her teammates left for the locker room, she slipped the notebook in her backpack. "Blaine, can we talk?" She tugged a towel around her shoulders and twisted the cap and goggles in her hand. A swim bag hung from her arm. "I was thinking. Maybe I could use my first-hour study hall for extra laps."

Coach Blaine stacked paddle boards on the pool deck. She had known him since third grade when she started swimming with the Waukesha Express Swim Team. "That's a lot of hours. You sure about that?"

"I want to do everything I can. I need to swim for a good college."

"You better talk to your parents." Coach Blaine never used a lot of words, so Gwen knew the conversation was over and what her next step should be.

At home, after her second swim practice, Gwen told Mom her idea.

"Shouldn't you use study hall for homework?" Gwen's mom raised one eyebrow as she set a plate of cheese and fruit on the table.

"I'll study at night. And Coach Blaine said he would stay to coach me." She smiled and pantomimed a prayer sign. "Please. I talked to my counselor. You just have to sign a release." Gwen handed her the form.

Mom sighed. "High school shouldn't be all work. What about time for fun? A movie or a dance?"

"Mom, I am having fun. My friends are all in the pool." Katie Mae swam at another high school, but Tristine, Allison and Gwen swam together every day at Waukesha South.

Tristine, Gwen, Allison with relay record

"I'll talk to Dad, but I'm not convinced this is a great idea."

Gwen went to her room, finished her algebra homework and pulled out a fresh sheet of paper. She drew columns with dates, times and classes, designing a homework schedule. She called her friend Kyle and arranged a carpool for morning practice. She pulled out her latest assignments with the As and Bs.

Persuasion in hand, Gwen found her mom and dad. "I've got some ideas," she said and showed them her papers.

"A carpool would make things easier," Mom said. "And we know you're a good student."

"Can I then?"

"We're concerned you spend too much time on one activity." Mom looked at Dad and he nodded.

"I'll still play violin. And go to religion on Wednesdays. And keep my grades up. I promise."

By the end of the conversation, Mom and Dad agreed to try it for a few weeks.

Gwen went to bed excited, convinced extra laps would improve her swimming.

Allison and Gwen

Gwen, Coach Blaine, Maggie Lach

CHAPTER 8

2001 Ninth Grade

At Waukesha South High School, as part of dry-land swim practice, Gwen jogged circles around the outdoor track. On the infield, football players yelled plays and threw passes. Yesterday, Gwen's swim team used elastic bands for shoulder work. Tomorrow, the weight room for legs and arms. Today, run laps for increased cardiovascular endurance.

As she breezed past the sand pit, Elizabeth screamed, "Go, Gwen!" Gwen looked away, wishing Elizabeth would get back to her own drills.

After a few sets, Gwen squirted water from the jug into a cup. When she looked up, Elizabeth's track coach, Eric Lehmann, was next to her. His hair stood up straight and he was eating something. He didn't remind Gwen of Coach Blaine at all.

"Hi, Gwen. Your sister says you're a good athlete. I think you should be running."

Why did he care about her? Why was Elizabeth talking about her? Gwen didn't enjoy the attention, so she looked for her teammates and tried to find a way out of the conversation. "I don't have time. I swim every day."

Each day that week, Eric found her. "Gwen, I mean it. You have talent."

He had tons of girls running. Why did he need her? "Thanks, but I don't think so."

"How about this?" he said. "You keep swimming—we'll call it cross-training. Don't even come to track practice. Just show up at a meet and run a race."

He offered her a pair of free running tights to practice in. He stopped at her house and talked to her parents.

The more Gwen thought, the more she wondered. Maybe Eric was right and she had talent. Maybe she could win a track race. She knew running was good for swimming. And the running tights looked cool. If she agreed to one event, perhaps he would stop asking. "Okay," she said. "Maybe one meet."

✢✢✢

That Saturday, Elizabeth helped Gwen sign in with the clerk of course. "Eric put you in the 800," Elizabeth said. "Good distance. Not a sprint, but not too long either."

The team started warm-ups—stretches, strides and leg swings. Gwen watched Elizabeth for what to do. Between drills, a teammate walked over to Gwen. "You took my spot and you didn't even show up to practice."

What could she say? Gwen just stared at her. She never thought running a race would make enemies.

"Let's hope you're worth it," the girl said. "No pressure." She flipped her hair and walked away before Gwen could answer.

Elizabeth leaned over and whispered. "Just don't worry about her. Have fun."

Even though Elizabeth could be loud and embarrassing, she always looked out for Gwen and tried to make her feel better.

When it was time for Gwen's race, the gun took her by surprise. The pace felt slow, so Gwen passed a few girls. Running felt easy. A few more girls dropped off and Gwen surged ahead. She liked the crowd cheering, whistles echoing as she ran past.

With a few meters to go, Gwen sprinted and won the race. She tried to act casual, but inside she was jumping up and down.

When she returned to the team area, Eric gave her a high five. "Good job, Gwen. Pretty impressive on your first try."

"Thanks."

"Keep this up and you'll be a real asset. Let's get you in a relay next week."

Gwen told Eric she was nervous about the girl who seemed to be envious.

"Ach, don't worry. She runs plenty of races."

Gwen kept swimming, kept skipping track practice and kept racing at track meets. She qualified for track sectionals and regionals. At the Wisconsin State Track and Field meet, she stood on the winners' podium. Fifth in the 800 meters. And fourth in the 4x800 relay.

She liked running, the ease of it, how she could train in the water and get good times on land. But in the pool, the world went quiet and Gwen felt at home.

Competing on a track relay

High school state swim

High school state track

CHAPTER 9

2001-2003 Tenth and Eleventh Grades

NCAA (National Collegiate Athletic Association) Division I teams were allowed to recruit high school juniors. The right letter or phone call could be the start of something big: a top university, a respected coach, talented teammates. Gwen imagined winning an NCAA finals event. Swimming at the Olympic trials. Making the Olympic team.

After one morning practice, she said, "Blaine, I really want to swim for Wisconsin or maybe Indiana or Notre Dame."

"Well, you sure work hard at it."

"What does that mean?"

"Think how many high schools there are in Wisconsin. Each one has an MVP like you. But there's only one UW-Madison and they take about eight new swimmers each year."

Coach Blaine didn't say she'd never won a state championship. But she knew that's what he was thinking. "So, do I have a chance?"

"You never know until you try."

Gwen asked every day—to swim more laps, to lift more weight and to meet with Waukesha Express Swim Team's sports psychologist. She convinced Blaine to help with her resume and make a video of her strokes.

Meanwhile, at conference events, Gwen swam distance freestyle and usually won. At more competitive races, she often took second or third.

"Good job, Gwen," Dad said in the car after she won a 500 freestyle race.

Gwen slouched in the passenger seat, remembering her slow start and terrible flip turns.

"What's wrong?"

"It wasn't a personal best. I can't just win. I have to get better."

CHAPTER 10

2003-2004 Twelfth Grade

At 6 p.m., Gwen pulled her car into the garage. Gwen hadn't been home in over 13 hours. Morning swim had started before the sun came up. Afternoon swim ended after dark. Although hungry and tired, she hurried in, knowing her mom left the mail on the kitchen table.

Last week, Gwen's friend Jenny received an offer from Madison. Jenny posted fast times this year and won an event at State last year. Were Gwen's stats good enough? Every day she hoped for an offer.

As she walked in the door, her mom said, "A letter came today."

Gwen grabbed the envelope and ripped it open. It looked official. She read the first line. Then, she looked at the letterhead. "It's nothing," she said, "Division III," and tossed it in the trash.

Later that week, more letters arrived. From Wisconsin colleges. Minnesota colleges. The U.S. Army. They praised Gwen's times at the Wisconsin State Track and Field Meet.

Her mom seemed excited when Harvard suggested a phone interview. "You could at least talk to them," she said. "Think of that—a Harvard education."

"Mom, it's for track. I'm a swimmer."

A few months earlier, Coach Blaine arranged a recruiting trip to Indiana University. Mom and Dad drove through a snowstorm so Gwen could meet the coaches. She was excited until she met the team. They were so tall, with broad shoulders and muscular arms. Standing next to them made her feel like a miniature doll. She wasn't surprised when, at the end of the trip, Indiana coaches made no offer.

Gwen focused on her first choice: the University of Wisconsin-Madison. Her parents followed Badger football, Coach Blaine swam there, and if she didn't receive an athletic scholarship, she would at least have the lower in-state tuition.

Gwen sent the Wisconsin coaches videos and her resume. And then, she waited and waited. After no response, Coach Blaine offered to place a call for both Gwen and Katie Mae and organize a meeting with the swim staff.

This was Gwen's chance. She planned her approach, gathered information, rehearsed what she would say. She knew her college career—and a chance at the Olympic Trials—depended on a good first impression.

At the meeting, Gwen asked lots of questions. She complimented the coaches and their team. She wanted them to feel her excitement, to know she was passionate and dedicated.

The coach said, "How about this? I can give you a walk-on spot."

This was it! Not a scholarship, but an in! She would be a college swimmer! Gwen wanted to high five him, to run up and hug him, but she held back. She didn't want to embarrass herself in front of her new coach.

The coach turned to Katie Mae. "We can offer you the same."

Katie Mae smiled so wide, Gwen thought her face might explode. She looked just like how Gwen felt. Ever since they joined Express, Gwen and Katie Mae moved together. This was the perfect next step. Gwen had her shot—she and Katie Mae would keep getting better together.

Gwen and Katie Mae enrolled at the University of Wisconsin-Madison for the fall of 2004. As walk-ons, they received no scholarship and had to prove they belonged—unlike recruited athletes, who were awarded money and prized for their talents. But Gwen didn't care. She was a Division I college swimmer.

Katie Mae and Gwen in their new University of Wisconsin-Madison sweatshirts

Gwen Wanted to Swim at a Division I School

The NCAA (National Collegiate Athletic Association) organizes colleges into three athletic divisions.

Typically, Division I schools have the largest undergraduate enrollments with the most funding and opportunities; there are more than 170,000 Division I athletes across 6,000 teams. Division I athletes can receive full athletic scholarships.

Division II athletes can receive partial athletic scholarships.

Division III athletes cannot receive athletic scholarships. With no roster limits, Division III usually has the most athletes.

Students at all three divisions can compete without a scholarship; in order to join an NCAA team, walk-on athletes typically go through a tryout. Although walking on is less common at Division 1 schools, Gwen walked on to all the UW-Madison sports she competed in: swimming and diving in 2005, 2006 and 2007; cross country in 2007 and 2008; and track and field in 2007, 2008 and 2009.

Gwen's Advice to Her Younger Self

Dear High School Gwen,

You are strong and independent. And yet, you still don't believe in yourself. Coaches and colleges say you're too small, too slow, too weak. Teammates set new personal bests, yet your times improve slowly. You worry about outcomes—position at meets, personal bests or state qualifications.

Don't think about achievements. They seem important, but sport should not define you. You are also a good friend, an outstanding student and a loving sister and daughter. Identify what you do well. You have so much to celebrate and be proud of.

Shift your focus to the process and to your technique. This is a different way of seeing sport. That's the path to success, to peace, to happiness. When you truly love the process, you'll smash what you think Is possible. You will discover your full potentIal—a potentIal you don't even know you have.

Sincerely,
Adult Gwen

CHAPTER 11

Rio 2016: Four Days Before the Olympic Triathlon

"I can't wait to test myself."

—Gwen Jorgensen

Gwen and Patrick landed in Rio de Janeiro, Brazil, and met the driver who would take them to their hotel. He hefted their bags into the trunk and offered water and snacks for the one-hour trip. "Most athletes stay in the village. But I have a hotel address. That right?"

"Yes. On Copacabana Beach," Gwen said. She was glad USA Triathlon chose this location. It was close to the triathlon course, away from the noise and activity of the Olympic Village.

When they arrived, hotel staff unloaded their bags. The temperature was 85° and a breeze blew through Gwen's shirt. Beachgoers in bikinis strolled the path between hotel and ocean. The air smelled salty and warm. Gwen checked the forecast on her phone: 80's and dry for August 20, the women's triathlon. Perfect for racing.

At their room, Patrick slipped the key in its slot and held the door while Gwen pulled in a few bags.

"Oh, my gosh! Patrick, look." USA Triathlon staff had decorated the room with an Olympic flag, a Team USA flag and red-white-and-blue garlands. There was a wrapped gift on the desk. It felt like being in high school or college when teammates decorated each other's lockers or doors. Gwen opened the gift—a set of earbuds. She thought of all the people cheering for her. She wanted to make each one proud.

"Gwen, I'm off to get food at the grocery store. Want anything special?"

When Gwen started racing triathlons in 2010, she discovered her body felt best with familiar foods. So, when traveling, Gwen and Patrick brought rice, oats, a rice maker, a knife and spoon. For produce and meat, there was usually a grocery store within walking or biking distance.

"Can you get avocado? And broccoli, please?"

Before he left, Patrick started some rice. Then, backpack over his shoulders, he took an elevator to the lobby.

While he was gone, Gwen unpacked her bags.

Following a concierge's directions, Patrick located a grocery store and returned with fresh vegetables, fruit and pre-cooked chicken. He also bought carbonated water to drink and still water for washing food and brushing teeth—they avoided tap water, which in some parts of the world can cause illness.

Patrick returned, and when the rice finished cooking, he put out a plate and added sliced chicken. He arranged a salad.

After they ate, Gwen journaled and answered emails while Patrick washed dishes. Then Patrick added water and oats to the rice maker. "We're all set for breakfast tomorrow," he said. "And I found bananas for you."

Gwen consumed a diet of protein, carbohydrates and vegetables. In meals, green was her favorite color, so Patrick used spinach, broccoli, asparagus, beans and avocado. She liked white rice because it was easy to digest and made her stomach feel good. She took in protein from eggs, steak and chicken.

Although Patrick planned to cook while in Rio, USA Triathlon hired Chef Adam and encouraged Gwen to eat with the other athletes. She felt nervous about eating unfamiliar dishes, so the next morning asked to speak to the chef.

Adam came out of the kitchen, wiping his hands on a white apron.

"Thanks for talking with me," she said. "I'm worried I won't feel well if I don't eat my usual meals."

Decorations in Gwen's Rio 2016 hotel room

"Yes. Athletes are particular about diet. As much as possible, give me requests and I will do my best to make them. And you should know we use strict safety measures."

Gwen and Patrick considered their options. Patrick could cook in their room, but relying on Chef Adam would save time during this important week. For this trip, they compromised. Sometimes Gwen ate the chef's food and sometimes Patrick cooked.

Gwen and Team USA's Chef Adam

Gwen's Favorite Breakfast Recipe

SWEET OR SAVORY OATS

<u>SERVINGS:</u> 1-2 professional athletes

INGREDIENTS
2 cups water or 1 1/2 cups water plus 1/2 cup full-fat milk
1/4 teaspoon salt
1 cup rolled oats
1-2 bananas, sliced

TOPPINGS
1/4 cup blueberries and/or walnuts (for sweet version) or
1-2 eggs, poached (for savory version)
1/2 cup full-fat or dairy-free milk
cinnamon to taste
salt to taste

DIRECTIONS
Method 1: In a medium saucepan, bring water and/or milk and 1/4 teaspoon salt to boil. Stir in rolled oats and bananas. Reduce heat and simmer uncovered for 15 minutes, stirring occasionally. Remove pan from heat; cover and let stand for 2 minutes. Add toppings.

Method 2: The night before, add boiling water and oats to a pot. (Do not use milk for this method.) Allow to sit overnight on the counter. In the morning, add salt and bananas and cook on the stovetop for 5 minutes, stirring occasionally. Remove from heat; cover and let stand for 2 minutes. Add toppings.

Oats can be made in a rice maker when traveling.

Why Gwen Doesn't Drink Tap Water

Contaminated drinking water can contain bacteria like E. coli, cholera and Salmonella. It may also carry Cryptosporidium or viruses like hepatitis A or rotavirus. Symptoms of illness range from mild stomach distress to serious disease.

To prevent illness, Gwen followed experts' advice. She drank bottled water and avoided ice cubes. In restaurants, she avoided raw vegetables since they may be rinsed in tap water.

Even bottled water calls for caution. The CDC (Centers for Disease Control and Prevention) says,

> Drinks from factory-sealed bottles or cans are safe; however, dishonest vendors in some countries may sell tap water in bottles that are "sealed" with a drop of glue to mimic the factory seal. Carbonated drinks, such as sodas or sparkling water, are safest since the bubbles indicate that the bottle was sealed at the factory. If drinking directly from a can, wipe off the lip of the can before your mouth comes into contact with it.

Gwen's Nutrition

For nutrition, Gwen concentrated on carbs, proteins, fats and fluids.

- **Carbohydrates.** Gwen loaded up on carbohydrates three to four days before a race. This built up her body's store of energy. Carbohydrates are in breads, cereals, pastas, fruits and vegetables.
- **Protein**. Gwen consumed protein from real foods rather than protein bars or drinks. Gwen's sources of protein included lean meats, fish, poultry, nuts, beans, eggs and milk.
- **Fat**. Gwen got her fat from a diet that includes nuts, avocados, olives, oils and fatty fish like salmon and tuna.
- **Fluid**. Gwen drank fluids before, during and after exercise. During competition, she drank to thirst, but made sure to sip at least every 15 to 30 minutes.

Gwen recommends athletes listen to their bodies. Eat when hungry. Drink when thirsty. And enjoy sweets in moderation. Gwen's favorite treat is one square of dark chocolate after most meals, even breakfast.

CHAPTER 12

2004-2006
Freshman and Sophomore Years at UW-Madison

At the University of Wisconsin-Madison, Gwen registered for general classes. She took art survey. She learned about writing and theater. She studied math and science and thought about being a nurse or an engineer. She signed up for accounting and was surprised when so many students dropped after the first class. She loved working with numbers, deciphering formulas, studying laws and regulations. She imagined herself at a cubicle, attending meetings with colleagues.

After talking with her parents, she applied to UW-Madison's School of Business as an accountancy major. Gwen needed an essay for the application. She jotted down a few ideas and called Elizabeth. "I'm still the worst on the swim team. Do you think there's a story there?"

"Well, what has that taught you?" Elizabeth, a writing teacher, helped her develop this essay:

Competitive: The Word That Defines Who I Am.

Ever since I was born, I have been trying to be the best at what I do; whether I am racing my sister around the block, aspiring to be the first chair violinist, or learning the most, I am in the fight until the end.

I am one of the worst swimmers on the University of Wisconsin-Madison competitive swimming team. When applying to colleges, I knew where I wanted to go and what I wanted to do, but just needed to persuade the coaches to let me on the team. After numerous emails and phone calls, the coaches learned who I was and decided to let me on the team; however, they had no idea the commitment they were about to get.

The first week of school we had an optional practice. I was the only freshman to show up, along with three other upperclassmen. Our swim coach gave us the hardest practice I ever had to swim through. The stroke of the day was butterfly—my weakest stroke. I was huffing and puffing, pulling my arms through the water as fast as they would go. Coach Geoff told me to go on a slower send-off because he saw me struggling. After five minutes on the slower send-off, I asked to be put back on with the older swimmers. He chuckled out, "Sure!" After practice ended, I pulled myself out of the water and staggered to the locker room to change. To my surprise, Coach Geoff was waiting for me as I exited. He said, "I thought I was going to have to go in and save you today, but you persisted to try to kill yourself. Your determination will pay off in the future." All I could do was smile and say, "Thanks." My body was aching; I had charley horses in both calves and was dreaming of sitting in a chair.

A year and a half later, I am still on the swim team. I am still not one of the best on the team; however, I have greatly improved. My competitive edge does not allow me to give up when times are difficult, which is why I believe I am fit to be a businesswoman. Balancing time for school, swimming, volunteering and social life is hard. However, I have found that when I need to get something done, I make time to do it and make sure I do it well. I never go into something without putting in one hundred percent.

Based on her grades and essay, the University of Wisconsin accepted Gwen into their five-year accountancy program. By the end of her fifth year, Gwen would complete an internship and receive her bachelor's and master's degrees. It would be stressful and a lot of work to balance swimming and studies. But making a plan with a known result settled her uncertainty and energized her.

***

On the swim team, everyone got faster while Gwen felt stuck. Katie Mae's butterfly improved. She scored points at the Big Ten Conference meet and qualified for the NCAA meet. The coach offered her a scholarship. Gwen was first in the water, last out, but her progress was slow. It seemed she would never go to the NCAA meet. The Olympic trials were definitely out. And she still had no athletic funding. So, she wrote a scholarship essay, "A Week of Winnings," and earned some money.

Gwen never did earn a scholarship for swimming. She received an academic scholarship, her parents helped with tuition and there would be a future opportunity she never predicted.

UW Coach Geoff Hanson and Gwen

Swim team door decoration

A Week of Winnings

Walking down State Street in Madison, Wisconsin, a red and white moped with a "WIN ME" sign caught my eye. I ran into the university bookstore and decided to fill out a sheet with my name, number, email, and address. My sister, Elizabeth, who happened to be with me at the time, saw that the box said, "Please only one entry per day." She suggested I enter my name every day until the drawing.

Once I got the idea in my head that I wanted to win, I was going to do everything I could to win. I have always had drive, motivation and an almost obsessive nature about things I wanted (which is why I've been swimming every day since I was thrown in a pool).

In the past, I've been told by my coaches, parents, and friends that I just need to relax and take a break. However, I think they underestimate the power of persistence: I won that moped, and not because I only entered once, but because I entered every day I could!

My phone rang on a Monday afternoon and when I answered, I was in disbelief. I had never won anything before. After that, the winnings started to roll in. The next day, I won a hot dog eating contest (six-and-a-half hot dogs in six minutes), and that Friday, I won a $50 gift certificate from a drawing our landlord was having. Since then, I haven't won much, but I continue to enter because persistence does pay off.

CHAPTER 13

2006-2007
Junior Year at
UW-Madison

By Gwen's third season as a University of Wisconsin swimmer, she improved a bit, but how did the others get so fast? What was their secret? She was proud of the team, but when her friends traveled to high-powered competitions, the apartment was so quiet. And solo laps in the pool felt like throwing a party where no one showed up.

She phoned her high school track coach to reminisce about running. "I kind of miss running," Gwen said to Eric Lehmann. She thought about looping the track, passing batons in relays.

"There's always the UW team. I'll talk to Stintzi."

Gwen's thoughts scrambled. "Wait, I'm not sure." She knew about the UW track and cross-country coach but didn't think Eric should call him. Being nostalgic wasn't a reason to join a collegiate team. It had been years since she ran every day. And she knew college track would be much more challenging than high school track. She tried not to think about balancing two practices, two travel schedules and school.

"I know you. You can do more in running than you can swimming. You have untapped talent."

Gwen agreed she could run faster than she did in high school. "Let me think."

When Katie Mae got home from class, Gwen asked, "Is this a good idea?"

"Gwen, why not? There's nothing to lose." Gwen trusted Katie Mae and liked the thought of exploring new potential. She could keep swimming and add track. It worked in high school.

She talked with her mom, dad and sister. Everyone seemed so sure she should give it a try.

Eric set up a time trial and Gwen ran 400s while Stintzi watched.

"We'd love to have you, if you're interested," Stintzi said. "As a walk-on, of course."

The season had already started and she had three years of eligibility. "I am." Gwen knew once she said it, she couldn't take it back.

A few weeks later, as Gwen prepared for her first college track race, Stintzi said, "Don't take the lead. Draft until the last lap." He said her goal wasn't to win. "Just do enough to qualify for finals." Gwen didn't understand. She never willingly relinquished a lead in the pool. How could she not give her best every race? She decided to see running as a journey or like an exploration. She would listen and trust her coach. She would learn how to maximize her talent.

UW Track and Field and Cross-Country Coach Jim Stintzi and Gwen

Gwen's Athletic Eligibility

According to the NCAA, "If you play at a Division I school, you have five calendar years in which to play four seasons of competition. Your five-year clock starts when you enroll as a full-time student at any college." Because Gwen participated in a five-year accountancy program, she had three years of eligibility when she started as a junior on the track and field team.

CHAPTER 14

2007-2009 Junior, Senior, and Master's Years at UW-Madison

Gwen went to a week of track and field practice—sometimes once a day, sometimes twice—while also attending swim practice.

Then her swim coach called and said he needed to talk. Her stomach felt skittish and jumpy. Gwen feared the meeting would be about her poor results.

The coach found her climbing out of the pool. "Thanks for meeting with me," he said.

She took off her goggles and cap.

"You've been swimming a long time."

She tried not to be scared.

"And we appreciate your effort."

She nodded, acknowledging her work hadn't scored points at meets.

"I talked to Coach Stintzi. He says you have potential in track."

Gwen nodded again.

The coach's words kept coming. "Do something you're good at...focus on running...give up swimming...no time to do both."

What would happen if she didn't swim? Her pulse felt panicky. It seemed her coach had already made up his mind.

"Gwen, I'm excited to see what you can do on land."

"I am too." Gwen said it and hoped she believed it. But it felt like she lost something. Like a part of her would disappear. If she weren't a swimmer, who would she be?

She told her mom, dad and Elizabeth she was excited but hesitant about switching to track. She made it seem positive. Gwen knew she could never be a top swimmer, and she might be a top runner, but it didn't erase her sadness.

***

On the track—her first season since high school—she made new friends. She learned about form and cadence. Running wasn't easy, but it felt natural. She met teammates who excelled in workouts, in analyzing the competition or in motivating the team. Everyone contributed and, here, Gwen contributed too.

As Gwen started to win races, a few scholarship athletes acted like she didn't deserve success so soon after joining the team—just like her high school teammates who thought she didn't deserve to cross-train in the pool and race on the track. That experience taught her not to worry about others' opinions. Naysayers were the minority. Most of her college teammates welcomed her and celebrated her successes.

After Gwen's first track season, Stintzi invited her to run cross country in the fall. Between seasons, she jumped in the pool for cross-training laps with Katie Mae. The water and strokes and scent of chlorine felt familiar and peaceful—but she was happy when she returned to land. On land, she saw progress; on land, she competed and won.

As her run times improved, Gwen approached Stintzi. "Coach, can we talk?" She was proud of her races and knew her performance bested many on the team. If the others were worth an athletic scholarship, she was too. "I think I deserve funding."

"That wasn't our agreement," he said.

"Are you willing to reconsider? I'm beating recruited athletes." It was only fair. She reminded him of her results—her indoor 3,000- and 5,000-meter Big Ten Championships; her All-American Cross Country finish; her school records.

Stintzi listened, reviewed his allotment of finances and awarded her a scholarship.

Now Gwen wanted to prove she deserved it. The season stretched before her, packed with races full of opportunity. Her goal: win the NCAA 5K Championship.

Gwen's Statements to the Press

My biggest challenge was waking up in the morning and trying to walk on my sore, underused leg muscles. During my first year of track my body was not used to pounding on land. It took a while for my muscles to develop and during that time I dreaded taking that first step out of bed in the morning and walking downstairs. Everything else was made easier because my teammates, coaches, and family supported me. Everyone helped me out during my transition, and I can't thank them enough!

Source: "Getting to Know Gwen Jorgensen, UW's Leading Cross Country Runner" November 05, 2008. Available: https://uwbadgers.com/news/2008/11/5/ Getting_to_know_Gwen_Jorgensen_UW_s_leading_cross_country_runner .aspx.

***

Although I miss the swimming team and coaches, I am thankful I made the switch, because the talented ladies and coaches I am surrounded by now are able to push me and the rest of my teammates to our potential.

Source: Rayford, Krysta. "Junior Picks Land Over Water." *The Badger Herald.* November 14, 2007. Available: https://badgerherald.com/sports/2007/11/14/ junior-picks-land-ov/.

Gwen's Collegiate Track Achievements

- Two-time first-team All-American in cross country and track and field
- Two-time Big Ten champion
- Three-time track NCAA Championship participant
- Two-time cross country NCAA Championship participant
- Six-time Academic All-Big Ten choice
- Big Ten Medal of Honor Recipient
- Member of the UW Athletic Hall of Fame

A post-race press interview

UW track yearbook

CHAPTER 15

Rio 2016: Three Days Before the Olympic Triathlon

"I focused on training and wrote my Rio race plan, which calmed my nerves."

—Gwen Jorgensen

Because Gwen competed in Rio for the 2015 Olympic test event, the 2016 week seemed familiar.

As she finished her morning oats, feet up in her bed, Gwen said to Patrick, "I like knowing where everything is. I feel prepared."

Patrick gave her a squeeze. "Are you anxious?"

"Not really," she said and hugged him back. "Just ready to race."

Every day, she ran, biked, swam, visualized, rested and took massage and physio treatments. When her family arrived in Rio, she didn't join them to visit the Cristo Redentor statue or Sugar Loaf Mountain. She didn't go samba dancing or enjoy a churrascarias (Brazilian steak) dinner. If she wasn't training or recovering, she rested, holed up like a hermit crab. With her Olympic race only days away, she aimed every thought on the start line.

Most days, she rode her bike on a trainer in her hotel room. It kept her off busy, dangerous roads. But three days before the race, at sunrise, the city closed streets for a preview. Patrick, Gwen and other athletes and teams rode the course.

"Patrick, let's do the incline again," she said.

Over and over, they rode the uphills and descents.

"Are you comfortable?" he said. "Do it as much as you want."

"I need a few more tries at the downhill." She took a pull from her water bottle. "To feel the turns."

After the course preview, it was time for a swim workout. At 10 a.m., she took an Uber to the pool where USA Triathlon rented lanes.

Gwen Competes in Olympic-Distance Triathlon

Triathlon is a race with three continuous sports. Athletes swim, then cycle, then run. The race is timed, including the transition between disciplines, and the fastest athlete wins.

The course includes a transition zone for gear. Athletes store their bikes in this area. It is also where they leave their swim goggles, cap and wetsuit and where their running shoes are pre-set.

The Olympic triathlon takes Gwen about two hours. It includes a
- 1.5-kilometer swim (about 20 minutes);
- 40-kilometer bike (about 70 minutes); and
- 10-kilometer run (about 35 minutes).

Other triathlon race formats include
- sprint—One-half the length of an Olympic-distance race (about 1 hour for elite athletes);
- Half Ironman or 70.3—The number indicates total miles traveled (about 4.5 hours for elite athletes); and
- Ironman—Also called 140.6 for total miles traveled (about 9 hours for elite athletes).

"Wanna change your mind?" Patrick said. "About practicing an ocean start?" Authorities warned about Zika virus in the ocean, but when tested, the waters passed competition standards.

"No. I made my decision. I can't control Zika, but I can control where I swim." Gwen reduced her risk of contracting Zika virus by preparing exclusively in the pool.

After her swim workout, she used neighborhood streets to run, eliminating a commute to the track or park. Then, with those saved minutes, she booked an extra massage.

CHAPTER 16

2009-2010 Master's Year and USA Triathlon

For three years, Gwen had been running track and cross country at the University of Wisconsin-Madison. She loved running. The long hours, alone in her head for 50 miles each week, felt like laps in the pool. And now that her sport better matched her body type, she found success in races.

Here she was, at the start line for her final collegiate track race—a 5K at the NCAA Finals in Arkansas. Her shin hurt. She iced it in the days leading up to the race, but it throbbed. Earlier that week, her coach wanted an X-ray, but Gwen refused. "After the race," she said. If a radiologist found even a hairline fracture, she wouldn't be allowed to run.

She might have dreamed of a running career but her times didn't meet professional standards. This was her last chance at a National Championship.

The starter called athletes to the mark. Two seconds of silence. Bang!

Gwen took off, slow on the start. She ran middle of the pack.

Her leg hurt more than she expected. A few passed her. A few more. Within seconds, 15 raced ahead.

Each step zapped her leg, a fiery current from heel to knee. She tried to catch up, to make herself go faster, to put determination over distress.

The front pack sped forward, graceful and quick. With each step, they increased their lead.

Gwen's pain intensified. She remembered swim events when she never gave up. She must stay in this race too.

Her leg recoiled with each step. She favored her good leg and sensed a limp. She couldn't avoid the reality of her injury and looked for a safe way to leave the track. It was the first time she dropped out of a race.

In the medical tent, the doctor said, "How long's this bothered you?"

"Few weeks. Coach thought I should get an X-ray," she said.

"He's right."

Gwen left the tent in a walking boot with instructions to see her doctor immediately after returning home. Her parents and Elizabeth said they were proud, but she felt defeated. She worked so hard, only to have an injury take her down. She had been the worst swimmer on the Madison team and now she didn't finish at her last NCAA track meet. She felt like a failure.

As she and her family walked toward the food tents, a woman with a clipboard and credentials on a lanyard joined them. "Hi, Gwen. Sorry to see the boot."

"Thanks. Me too. Mom, Dad, Elizabeth, this is Barb Lindquist." Barb was a 2004 Olympic triathlete. Now, she worked for USA Triathlon's Collegiate Recruitment Program identifying men and women with triathlon potential.

"Gwen, I hope you're considering triathlon. With your talent, you could be on the Olympic team." When Gwen didn't know what triathlon was, Lindquist had explained the two-hour race of swim, bike, run.

"I tried to be an Olympian. I'm not that good. And I have my accounting job at Ernst & Young."

"Just give it a shot. If you don't like it, you don't like it." Lindquist said she would send Gwen a bike, free of charge, and find her a coach, also free. "We'll take it one day at a time. You give it some thought and I'll call next week."

Gwen wanted to stay in shape. She planned to run once her leg healed. And she wouldn't mind a few sessions in the pool. Learning to bike would be a challenge, but it might be good cross-training. Lindquist said most expenses would be covered by the recruitment program, so Gwen didn't have to worry about the cost.

When Lindquist called, Gwen reluctantly said yes. "But my job comes first. And I'll have to train in Milwaukee where I'm working." Probably nothing would come of triathlon, but it was exciting to think about an Olympic quest. And flattering that Barb considered her talented.

Dad, Gwen at The Bean in Chicago

Since childhood, Gwen swam in a pool. Now, she had to learn open water swimming—with a wetsuit in Lake Michigan.

Her new road bike was a mystery. When to shift gears? How to shift gears? How to unclip shoes from the pedals? Gwen knew she would learn from being on a team, so she joined a cycling group for weekly rides.

One day, a rider pulled next to her. "Hi, Gwen. I'm Tom." She discovered later he was Tom Schuler, 1976 and 1980 Olympic cyclist. "You're new?"

"Just learning," she said as they approached a stop sign.

Tom unclipped his shoe from the pedal, glided to a stop and put his foot on the pavement. Gwen wiggled her shoe

A 2010 triathlon

and tried to release it, but she couldn't get it out. Losing momentum as she braked for the stop sign, her shoe stuck in place and she tipped over.

"Ride with me," Tom said. "I'll help."

Every week after that, Tom found Gwen and coached her. He taught her to look up the road instead of at the ground. To give herself time to shift gears before attacking a hill. To pull up on her pedal as well as push down. To shift her weight over the saddle. To use drop bars for balance. To keep her hands near the brake levers. To unclip well before stop signs.

As Gwen trained, she checked in with Barb, sending written reports and asking questions. Barb became Gwen's mentor, encouraging and advising her. After a few months, Barb said, "Gwen, I think you're ready for racing."

Gwen wasn't sure. She felt uncertain and timid on the bike. But she trusted Barb and agreed to try.

At her first race, an elite development event, she lagged in the swim and fell further back in the bike. But with her running, she made up time, placed in the top ten and earned her pro card. It was only ten months since she started triathlon. She was proud of her achievement but reminded herself this was the least competitive professional race.

Barb scheduled more races and Gwen's training and effort led to a silver at the World University Triathlon Championships in Spain. She was USA Triathlon's Rookie of the Year and Duathlete of the Year. She liked the feeling of winning and wanted to do more, but she explained to reporters how many mistakes she made and how much she still had to learn.

What didn't I learn this year? I had no idea how to mount a bike at my first triathlon, and at my second triathlon, I left a bag of rubber bands in my shoes at T2. Every race, and every practice, I was learning something new...Athletes were willing to help me at races, and were always pointing out areas where I could improve—whether it be where to sit in a pack, how to ride over cobblestone, or which spot to pick when lining up for the swim...

With training, working and competing, the days exhausted Gwen. She swam before dawn, worked as an accountant until dark, ran after dinner and biked on a trainer before bed. On weekends, she cycled with Tom Schuler's group or traveled to a race. She kept a planner and organized her schedule. She asked Ernst & Young if she could sometimes work remotely. For a while, she managed to do it all. But how could she continue? Her stomach hurt from stress, she didn't have time to take in adequate calories and she couldn't sleep.

Gwen and Elizabeth at NCAA meet

Gwen Used Cycling Shoes

Gwen with her road bike

Cycle shoes and pedals work together. Connecting them with a bolt system allows the cyclist to both push down and pull up on the pedals. This generates power.

When stopping, the cyclist releases the shoe by twisting the foot. During early rides, Gwen often failed to release her shoe. Unable to use her foot for balance as she slowed down, she tipped over. After practicing the move over and over, she learned to unclip easily.

Gwen Earned a Pro Card

To compete as an elite, athletes need a license, also called a pro card. To earn a pro card, athletes must apply to USA Triathlon and meet one of several criteria. Gwen earned her card at the 2010 Clermont Elite Development Race because she met "CRITERIA F: Finish top-3 overall in the amateur field at an Elite Qualifying Race."

Gwen's ITU Olympic-Distance Races

The International Triathlon Union (ITU) governs the sport of triathlon and sanctions World Triathlon Series (WTS), World Cup (WC) and Continental Cup (CC) races. Gwen raced all of these during her career.

- Continental Cup events offer smaller prizes and fewer points; these races are for young or inexperienced athletes.
- World Cup events are more competitive than Continental Cup races, but less competitive than WTS races; with top WC finishes, athletes earn ITU, WTS and Olympic points.
- World Triathlon Series is where the world's best triathletes compete to be named World Champion. Athletes can earn points for each race (both in the Olympic and sprint distances), with higher finishers earning more points. In 2019, there were eight stops in the World Triathlon Series.
- Pan American Games occur the year before the Olympics for athletes from North, Central and South America and the Caribbean.

Gwen's Advice to Her Younger Self

Dear Triathlete Gwen,

You're a professional triathlete. Wow! You didn't see this coming. But now you want to be the best. You've always wanted to be the best. To get there, look to the top women. What are they doing on a daily basis? Notice, make a plan and work to improve. When you figure out what you need, your training will change completely.

Find a lesson in every experience. London will show you can perform even when sick and fatigued. Gold Coast will teach you to train for a specific course. Stockholm will show you're the whole package.

In triathlon, and in life, identify what you can control. Learn to prepare and adjust. To mitigate risk. To increase the likelihood of success, of winning the race because of what's inside you—your engine. Then you will become a true triathlete, leader and role model.

Gwen, be bold. Announce your goals to the world. That will hold you accountable. And then, you'll start winning. But you know what? For once, you won't care. You won't care because you're realizing your potential.

Sincerely,
Adult Gwen

CHAPTER 17

2011 Patrick Lemieux

Gwen rode toward the back of Tom Schuler's Saturday bike group. The Texas Roadhouse Cycling team, a group of professional cyclists visiting Milwaukee for the Tour of America's Dairyland races, led.

One of them slowed and pulled next to her. "Hi. I'm Patrick."

"Hi," she said. He was so cute. And that smile! "I'm Gwen."

"Tom says I might be able to help. You're working on racing?"

"For triathlon."

Throughout the two-hour ride, Patrick coached Gwen. When she tired, he encouraged her and led her back into the pack. It was the first time she completed a ride in Tom's group without getting dropped. Patrick smiled at her and Gwen smiled back, even though her legs burned and her heart pounded.

As they cycled slowly to their cars, Patrick said, "Wanna get dinner?"

Gwen knew he was asking her on a date. She told herself she didn't have time for a boyfriend. But he was so tall and friendly and good-looking and...maybe just one dinner. She said yes and then couldn't believe Patrick rode no-handed to type her number into his phone. She was charmed by his easy manner and interest in her. "Yes," she said, "but not too late. I have to work early tomorrow."

After that week, Patrick visited Milwaukee many times to join Gwen for bike rides and dinner. He showed her how to shift, how to attack a hill and how to descend. Then, after their sessions, he explained when to adjust a chain or how to clean her bike. Gwen found him patient, empathetic and kind. She was happy when he asked her to be his girlfriend. She felt at peace when she was around him. And when Patrick returned to his home in Minnesota, she talked with him on the phone, sometimes long into the night when she knew she should have been asleep.

Patrick (center) on cycling brochure

Gwen's Statement to the Press

With Patrick, I would be checking my phone every minute, hoping for his phone call. I never thought I would feel how Patrick makes me feel. He walks in the room and I instantly smile. He makes me laugh, he is always there to bounce ideas off of, and he loves me more than I thought possible. I can't imagine life without him, and I have tried to force him to promise he won't die before me. He just says, 'I can't promise that, but I can try.' With him, life is so much better. He makes me a better person.

Source: Shaw, Jené. "V-Day Special: Behind Gwen Jorgensen's Proposal." *Triathlete*. February 14, 2014. Available: https://www.triathlete.com/culture/v-day-special-behind-gwen-jorgensens-proposal/.

CHAPTER 18

2011-2012 Training in Wisconsin

Most days, Gwen got up at 4 a.m. for a swim at the YMCA Walter Schroeder Aquatic Center. By 8 a.m., she sat at her Ernst & Young desk calculating corporate taxes. At 6 p.m., she biked or ran or swam again. On weekends, she traveled to competitions. With little time to relax, her sleep was fitful and never enough.

Her triathlon coach, Cindi Bannink, lived in Madison, Wisconsin, about 90 minutes from Gwen's Milwaukee apartment. Cindi wrote workout plans and communicated via email, phone and text. After each race or week of training, Gwen composed reports and emailed them to Cindi and Barb Lindquist.

Gwen was always tired and nothing received full attention: not work and not her Olympic triathlon pursuit. She scheduled a meeting with her boss. She needed time off but was nervous about letting down her co-workers and what her boss might say. She called her mom after the meeting.

"He was so nice!" she said. "I can reduce my hours and come back full-time whenever I'm ready."

"That's great," her mom said. "Dad and I can help with money then."

"No! I want to do this on my own."

"But what about rent? And swim fees? And food?"

"I've saved and I think I have a Timex sponsorship. Plus, USAT will help with race fees and travel costs."

Gwen and her parents knew she could always go back to accountancy; the same wasn't true for athletics. It was a risk to reduce her income and pursue an Olympic spot, but one Barb and Cindi—and Gwen's gut—convinced her to take.

Gwen forced herself not to worry about the unknowns—the bones she could break, the muscles she could tear, the money it could cost. Instead, she thought about her potential and what she might discover. She made lists, formulated a plan and set a goal: qualify for the London 2012 Olympics.

With Barb Lindquist in Florida

Florida transition zone

Getting ready for Florida race

Gwen Learned Triathlon's Rules

The International Triathlon Union (ITU) publishes a rule book that is frequently updated. It regulates athlete conduct and sportsmanship, anti-doping, athletic wear, race numbers, timing, penalties, and equipment for each discipline of swimming, cycling and running.

Race officials enforce rules. They include the chief race official, the head referee and the technical officials. These men and women are assigned to monitor registration, start, finish, transition areas, pre-transition area, swim, swim exit, bike, run, wheel stations, aid stations, technology, penalty boxes, lap counter, protocol, race control office, video review and vehicle control.

Coaches and mentors helped Gwen learn the rules. In one race, she racked her bike incorrectly and served a 15-second penalty. Then, experience was her teacher.

CHAPTER 19

2011–2012 European Circuit

As Gwen trained in Milwaukee for triathlon, she reduced her work hours and eventually took a leave of absence from Ernst & Young. She devoted more and more time to workouts, traveling and competing. She made a public announcement about her bid for the London 2012 Olympic team.

Her early results were inconsistent: 3rd in Clermont, Florida; 5th in Mazatlan, Mexico; 16th in Mooloolaba, Australia. She realized she couldn't win right away and trusted that practice and coaching would improve her finishes.

"Mom, Dad, you set for London and Tiszaújváros?" During the summer of 2011, Gwen's parents would travel with her to England and Hungary. "But, don't expect much. Barb says it's just for experience."

Including Gwen, USA Triathlon sent five female triathletes to the London 2011 triathlon. It was a qualifying event for next year's London 2012 Olympics. If USA athletes finished in the top nine, they would automatically be on the Olympic team. Gwen was ranked 54th. For her, top-20 would be a victory.

On the cold, damp August race day, Gwen had a mediocre swim and missed the front bike pack. Then, the leaders lost their advantage and everyone formed a single pack.

Gwen dismounted, heart storming, lungs searing. She racked her bike, deposited her helmet and slipped on her running shoes. She could relax now. She felt relieved the swim was over. And thankful she made it through the bike without a crash. All she had to do was run—the easy part.

In the first run lap, she moved from 45th to 17th. So much easier than battling waves and flailing arms and legs. In the second and third laps, she moved to the top ten. So much nicer than riding within an inch of someone's wheel.

Gwen caught up to one of her USA teammates. "C'mon, Laura, we can do this."

Laura Bennett finished fourth in the Beijing 2008 Olympics. But Laura looked tired. She tapped Gwen's butt and said, "Go get 'em, girl."

So, Gwen ran ahead. And passed a few runners. And a few more.

Approaching the finish line, Gwen saw only Helen Jenkins from Great Britain ahead of her. Could she really be in second place? Ahead of all the USA athletes? Someone handed her an American flag. How do you hold this and run? Which way is up? Should it be in front? Or in back? It hardly seemed real when she crossed the finish line with over 50 athletes behind her.

The race played perfectly to her strengths and Gwen felt lucky. She never expected to be on the podium. Or to qualify this soon for the London 2012 Olympics! It didn't seem real.

An official led Gwen and the other medalists to the podium. She accepted the silver medal—the best finish ever for a USA triathlete in a World Triathlon Series race. She stood at attention while Great Britain's national anthem played. She opened a champagne bottle and sprayed. She waved to her parents in the grandstand.

The aftermath became a maze—Gwen navigated one path and found three more to figure out. Drug testing. Fans requesting autographs. Reporters firing questions: *How long have you been racing? Did you expect to qualify? Can you win next year at the Olympics?*

She didn't anticipate the attention. Or cameras. Gwen disliked public speaking and now international reporters asked questions and wrote down everything she said.

After London, Gwen and her parents traveled to Hungary for her next race. Again, she made up time on the run and, in the chute, an official handed her an American flag. She still didn't know how to hold it. But she crossed the line with it, this time in first place. More questions followed from reporters, coaches, agents, athletes. It felt like someone aimed a floodlight at her and then demanded answers—all about swim, bike, run.

When Gwen returned home, The United States Olympic Committee (USOC) flew her to Los Angeles for a photo shoot. She appeared on a late-night television show. She sat for interviews. She trained. In just a few months, her life changed from tax accountant to full-time Olympic athlete.

Media focused on Gwen—how she came out of nowhere to beat experienced triathletes, how she took second on the Olympic course—and it felt like she was expected to repeat.

She had so many questions about the Olympics, the US Olympic Committee, rules, promotion, funding, training. She trusted Barb and Cindi for guidance and decided to not worry about factors out of her control. Instead, she concentrated on her race preparation.

Champagne celebration after London 2011 race

Gwen Raised the USA Flag

It's sometimes considered poor sportsmanship to high-five fans or celebrate during competition. However, in triathlon, it is a tradition for athletes to carry their country's flag as they approach the finish line. A pre-finish celebration is also common in endurance sports like the marathon.

The first two times Gwen was handed a USA flag during competition, she wasn't sure how to carry it. Later, USA Triathlon emailed her the protocol. Gwen learned to raise the flag horizontally above her head, hold the square of stars in her right hand and the stripes in her left, and allow it to billow behind her.

Gwen Answered Interview Questions

Sometimes athletes answer questions for individual reporters. Other times, they field questions from groups of reporters. In high school, college, and the professional world, Gwen's coaches advised her on media interactions. She prepared to
- know her message,
- be truthful,
- anticipate questions,
- have answers ready, and
  say only what she wanted on the record.

CHAPTER 20

2012 London Olympics

With qualification accomplished, Gwen focused on training for the London 2012 Olympic race. She tried to ignore the media chatter. The writers who said she couldn't win. The ones who expected her to.

She needed race experience, so she competed in Florida, USA (6th); Sydney, Australia (4th); San Diego, USA (51st); and Banyoles, Spain (1st).

There was so much to learn. How to hydrate and take in nutrition; avoid getting pushed underwater; quicken her transitions; bunny hop over a pothole; gain speed pedaling barefoot; respond to a breakaway; maneuver slick roads; ride on cobblestones.

She picked up a few tricks: spray with cooking oil to make a wetsuit slide off; use rubber bands to hold shoes in place on the racked bike; position in the front of a pack to avoid crashes. Then, ready or not, the London Olympic race arrived.

On August 4, 2012, Gwen's mom and dad watched from the grandstand in London's Hyde Park. Elizabeth and Patrick found a spot on the street. Gwen didn't see her parents or Elizabeth before her race; she concentrated on the triathlon.

Gray skies blew mist on the athletes and coated every London surface. Patrick had adjusted Gwen's tire pressure for wet roads.

Gwen's mind was a mix of confidence and uncertainty. She remembered her silver medal from last year, but she was still so new to the sport. And the Olympic experience was unlike any other, with additional security measures and requirements to check bikes and clothing. She felt like it was the first day of school, eager to give things a try, but anxious about her readiness.

She lined up for the swim and dove into the murky Serpentine—a recreational lake in the park. For 20 minutes, she stayed in a pack and exited in 24th place. Not a terrible swim. She'd had worse.

Already, a lead cycle group, which included USA teammates Laura Bennett and Sarah True, formed. Gwen joined a chase pack. During the first lap, she tried to get a feel for the pavement, but she rode cautiously. She saw a cyclist sprawled on the ground—someone crashed. Don't get distracted, she thought. Pay attention. White painted lines were everywhere, slippery like ice in the light rain. Don't lose concentration, she told herself, even for a second.

Then something seemed off. Was it the damp road? Was the asphalt different? Was her brake dragging? It almost felt like a flat tire. No—it couldn't be. Gwen turned to the rider next to her. "Do I have a flat?"

The woman glanced and nodded. "Yes."

Maybe she was wrong. "Are you sure?"

"You have a flat."

Where is the wheel station? How far? Then what? She tried to remember how the exchange worked. She had never experienced a flat in competition.

She exited the course to a white tent filled with racks of equipment. She had to do this fast. She knew no one would help. Her mind raced, searching for information—what did Patrick say about derailleurs, chains, cogs, nuts?

As she entered the wheel exchange, an official monitored her entry. "What kind of wheel do you need?"

Gwen wasn't sure how to answer. She was still learning the mechanics of her bike. "The back one?"

It seemed to take so long. Riders zoomed past. She was losing time. She needed to stop her fingers from shaking. Her stomach felt twitchy. How many minutes was she losing? She had to hurry. She released the flat, lined up the fresh wheel, locked it in and attached the chain. She rotated the pedal to check the derailleur. Satisfied the wheel was safely installed, she dashed to the course, bike under her palm, and mounted.

Where was she? How far back? The important thing was to keep racing. To focus on what she could control. To finish.

She pressed into one pedal. Pulled up on the other. She had lost momentum and now labored to invent it. This race felt like a bad dream, pedaling fast and going nowhere.

After riding solo for a few minutes, Gwen spotted Canadian Paula Findley, who had won several WTS races, leading a pack. Gwen increased her speed and latched on. At least now she had the momentum of a group. The women shared the lead and Gwen surprised herself, feeling like one of the stronger cyclists as they worked together.

Passing through the grandstand on the next lap, she glanced at the timing clock. A five-minute deficit. I can't worry. Get through the bike. Make up time on the run.

She finished the bike leg with the leaders far out of sight.

Gwen's running had won previous races. She hoped for the same now. How many athletes could she pass? She wouldn't know until she tried. On lap one, she overtook a few. Think about form, she thought. Second lap, a few more. Third lap, more. Shoulders down. Drive the arms. Be light on the feet.

During the fourth and final lap, with no idea how far behind she was, she spied Japan's Ai Ueda a few paces ahead. I can beat her! Sprint!

Almost to the finish line, using Ai as a target, Gwen accelerated. At that moment, place didn't matter. It was Japan versus USA. Gwen gained advantage. Ai responded. They battled, stride for stride. This is what the Olympics are about, Gwen thought. To do my best.

Gwen's race tattoo

After two hours, six minutes and 34 seconds, Gwen beat Ai to the line and finished 38th.

Gwen walked off the course and looked for her coach, Cindi. Words wouldn't form, but tears did. As they quietly walked to retrieve Gwen's bike, Patrick, Elizabeth and her parents trailed behind. Gwen's chest felt tight and there was a pain in her throat. She worked so hard, did everything her coach said, and fate handed her a flat tire. She knew she would spend days reliving the race—her decisions, what should have gone differently—and feeling the sadness, disappointment, frustration.

But something inside said, I was so close. Without a flat tire, I could have been a contender. I have four years to get this right. To win gold at the Rio 2016 Olympics.

Patrick and Gwen

Cindi and Patrick post race

CHAPTER 21

2012 The Gwen and Patrick Team

Gwen and Patrick had been dating for more than a year. They enjoyed time together, whether for recreation or work. They frequently rode their bikes, Patrick coaching Gwen on technique and race strategy. One day, Patrick said, "Gwen, I think I can help even more."

"What do you mean?"

"You concentrate on training and racing." He leaned in and touched her arm. "I'll be your full-time shopper and chef and assistant."

This was a surprise. An idea Gwen never considered. Her mind whirred. Had Patrick considered his own life? How it would change? What about his bike races? His job in Minnesota? "But what about cycling?" she said. "You can't just give that up."

"I'll never be as good at cycling as you are at triathlon. I want us to do this. Together."

After several discussions, Gwen was willing to try. She wasn't sure how every detail would work, but Patrick could help with so much. Not only the cooking and shopping, but travel plans and social media posts and navigating foreign countries. And it would be nice to have him around when she felt overwhelmed or frustrated or lonely.

Gwen and Patrick

Funding Gwen and Pat

In 2011, Timex paid Gwen an $8,000 annual salary and provided her with a swim kit and wet suit. David Hobbs Honda gave her a car. Team USA paid for coaching, accommodations and travel.

By 2016, Gwen's agent had advocated for her worth and negotiated contracts, procuring sponsorship from ASICS, Specialized, Columbia Threadneedle, Island House, ROKA, Oakley, Red Bull, Sleep Number, Pete and Gerry's Organic Eggs and TrainingPeaks. Gwen only accepted sponsorship from companies whose products she trusted and used.

During the 2016 race season, five sponsors paid Gwen between $5,000 and $20,000 to have their name on her race suit. Other sponsors supported her with cash or products. In return, Gwen endorsed their companies, posted about them on social media and made appearances. Gwen earned additional income from race winnings and sponsor bonuses

Gwen's Statement to the Press

"I don't do anything when I'm training, besides emails and sleeping," said Jorgensen, who believes that she went to the grocery store only once or twice during the 2015 season.

Source: "Happy Wife, Happy Life," Seth Rubinroit. NBC Sports. Available: https://sportsworld.nbcsports.com/gwen-jorgensen-triathlon-husband-patrick/.

Patrick's Statement to the Press

In the last year, we've spent maybe 361 days together. Most of those days, we're generally together from sunrise to sunset and in between. I'm sure we drive each other crazy, but that's what we signed up for. People often ask me if I ever get resentful that it's about Gwen all the time. And I'll tell them that if this was my designated job for 30 years, maybe. I can see how someone might get burnt out. But the lifestyle that we live—all the travel and the rigors of the sport—is very easy for me to handle because we know there's an end date. We just don't know when it is. Realistically, after Rio, the most she can do is four more years. What we're doing right now is creating a foundation of values and saving money. If you finish your sports career as a homeowner, you can be thankful.

Source: Goyanes, Cristina. "Why I Quit My Career to Become a House Husband for My Wife." *Women's Health*. May 10, 2016. Available: https://www.womenshealthmag.com/fitness/a19995809/gwen-jorgensen-patrick-lemieux/.

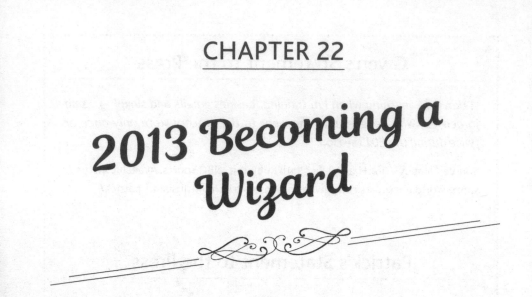

CHAPTER 22

2013 Becoming a Wizard

Gwen wanted redemption after her poor result in London. She wanted to test and challenge herself, to realize her potential and discover how well she could perform without a flat tire.

On social media, she posted her goal: "I want to go to Rio and I want to win gold." She talked with teammates, coaches, friends and family. Saying it made her accountable.

But something had to change. She needed more intensive training. In Wisconsin, her coach lived an hour away, and the people she trained with weren't on an Olympic journey. She studied top triathletes and noticed they collaborated in daily performance environments.

Gwen researched groups and interviewed coaches, including New Zealander Jamie Turner. "Do you think I can be the Olympic champion?" she asked him.

"You need to swim faster," Jamie said. "You need to bike faster. You probably need to run a 32-minute 10K." Jamie led the Wollongong Wizards, a co-ed team of international triathletes. "And, what would you bring to our group?" He expected each athlete to contribute.

Gwen remembered that even as the worst on her college swim team, she modeled long hours in the pool, hosted recruits and cheered for top performers. "I'll work as hard as anyone on your squad."

"It's more than hard work," Jamie said. "You have to be a leader."

Gwen and Patrick discussed the potential move. They considered the Wollongong Wizards the best in the world. But training with Jamie meant moving to Australia, and then to Spain, leaving family and friends and all Gwen's favorite places. It was a huge and expensive risk.

Gwen talked with her parents. She was scared about being so far from them. Whenever she was sick or needed help, they were an hour away. It would take 24 hours to fly to Australia. And what about money? She had the help of an agent now, but was her sponsorship enough to pay the bills? What about Australia's high cost of living? The expense of flying to races? She had a year or two in savings from her accounting job, but how long would that last? What would training be like? Would the Wizards welcome her? Could she fulfill Jamie's expectations? She laid out her options. She aired concerns. Listed advantages.

If she wanted to reach her goal, there was no other choice. She would join Jamie and the Wollongong Wizards.

On January 1, Gwen and Patrick flew to Australia. They wouldn't return to the US until October.

***

In Australia, Gwen and Patrick worked together to figure out schedules and routines. "What can I do?" he said after breakfast the first day.

"Well, I have a swim workout this morning, so maybe have lunch ready when I'm done?"

Each day after breakfast, Patrick hopped on his bike for the grocery store. He bought rice and vegetables and then pedaled to the meat shop. He introduced himself to the butcher and learned about the best cuts of beef and pork. Back home, he made lunch. He asked Gwen for feedback. She told him what foods agreed with her and the quantities she needed.

Gwen also counted on Patrick to clean the apartment and wash clothes. To make travel reservations, compose ideas for her interviews and communicate with her agent. With Patrick's help, Gwen had extra time for recovery. She took a nap every day and scheduled massages and physiotherapy appointments. When Gwen and Patrick talked, she shared her successes or frustrations. Patrick, who had competed professionally, understood the ups and downs, the pressure and the self-doubt. He was such a good listener and advice-giver and problem-solver. Gwen thought they made a good team. Patrick gave Gwen an advantage most athletes didn't have.

***

In training, Jamie told Gwen not to worry about results. He said the year would be about skill development.

"It feels strange not to think about winning," Gwen said to Patrick. "Not sure I can do that. But Jamie's right about one thing. I need to get better. In everything."

With Jamie's help, Gwen set process-driven goals: specific targets for each facet of her race. She focused on cadence in her run, arm position in her swim, shifting and power on her bike. They never discussed how to win an event. Jamie told Gwen if she did all the little things right, results would follow.

Then, at her first race since joining the Wizards, Gwen took the silver medal. She was surprised, but reminded herself it was only a Continental Cup, not a World Cup or World Triathlon Series race. A podium finish at this lower level was like jumping from the edge of the pool while the best athletes attempted the high dive. She put the silver medal out of her mind, considered it a fluke and re-focused on skill-building.

Two months later, at a World Triathlon Series race, she dove into the 62° ocean from a wharf in New Zealand. It was so cold! No matter how hard she stroked, she couldn't warm up. On the bike, the 60° wind whipped against her dripping suit. It felt like frost. She could barely push the pedals. Her legs wouldn't move. Her fingers cramped. How could she be dead last? Where was everyone? Was she going the right way?

Gwen passed Jamie where he stood on the side of the road. "Pull off the course!" he shouted.

Later, Gwen explained in her blog what happened:

I got to the race and made a mistake. I was cold to begin with, and I did a swim warm-up, thinking if I changed suits, I would be fine and warm back up. This wasn't the case. I ended up shaking/very tense for the half hour I was standing, waiting for the race to start. I knew others were cold too, you could see it in their bodies. I didn't think much of it, as I assumed as soon as I hit the water, I would warm up. I dove in and gave it all I had in that moment and found myself moving backwards and not warming up. I shifted my focus to processes; however, this didn't seem to help as I exited the water nearly last. I got to my bike and could barely mount. I started pedaling and felt like I was riding a bike I'd never been on before. It was the strangest feeling. At one point in the race, I thought I was going the wrong direction on the course—a bit delusional, perhaps? I ended up pulling out of the race.

Gwen had suffered from hypothermia. Her ultra-thin frame couldn't stay warm in the frigid water and air. All energy went to warming her body and nothing remained for competing.

In the weeks that followed, Jamie and Gwen brainstormed solutions and made a plan: avoid events with extremely cold water; eliminate water warm-ups in favor of dry land exercises; hire a company to design a battery-operated warming jacket. Gwen was beginning to learn from her mistakes and adjust factors within her control.

***

When the Wizards transitioned to Spain for warmer weather and proximity to races, Gwen targeted her swim—a faster time in the water would put her in a lead bike pack. Next season, she would target her cycling—a faster time on the bike would put her in a lead run pack.

Regardless of Jamie's emphasis on process over winning, Gwen scored top marks. On April 19, 2013, in San Diego, California, with her parents and Elizabeth in the stands, she won a World Triathlon Series race.

Not only did she win, Gwen was the first USA athlete ever to win a World Triathlon Series race. It gave her confidence. She was on the right path. She was in the right place: with Jamie and the Wizards, on her way to Olympic gold.

Then, she won another World Triathlon Series event in Japan and one more in Sweden. By the end of the season, Gwen Jorgensen was in a virtual tie for the World Championship. Now, she only had to win once more at the Grand Final race.

If she beat the other two women at the top of the points tally, she would be 2013 World Champion. No one expected this kind of quick success—especially Gwen.

The September 14, 2013, Grand Final was set for Hyde Park in London, the same course where, one year ago, she had a flat tire. The stakes were top prize money; the potential for high-level sponsorship; the prestige of a World Championship trophy.

Gwen exited the Serpentine River with the top 14. A quick transition (6th fastest) put her in the front bike pack. She later described the bike leg in her blog:

> *Wetsuit off. Helmet on. Bike mounted. Now, it was time for me to find some good wheels. Non [Stanford] was right there, along with Ashleigh Gentle. There were a lot of strong girls who quickly formed a group of about 20. I was riding in good position, and feeling comfortable on the bike. The rain started to fall and the temperatures began to drop.*
>
> *Then it all went wrong. I wish I knew what happened, but all I remember is being on the ground. I don't remember a thing. Someone said I may have stood up, but I watched the replay and it didn't look that way to me. I don't remember grabbing my brakes. I had the best equipment. My tire pressure was low (70 psi). And everything we did prepared me for the best possible outcome; however, I ended up dazed, confused, and in a bit of shock. I remember getting back on my bike and thinking, Ouch, my hands hurt. I looked at the palms of my hands, but they weren't even red. Strange. You must be fine. OK, you know a group is coming, along with the Anne Haug train. Just stay focused. You are still in this!*
>
> *The next thing I knew, two groups had come and gone. I remember some girls yelling words of encouragement, but nothing worked. I had to call it a day.*

Patrick met her as she walked off the course. "Let me see the bike." He lifted up the handlebars and spun the front wheel. He checked the back wheel. "The bike seems fine."

Gwen wanted to blame the bike, and when she couldn't, they both cried. "My whole body hurts."

Patrick wrapped her in a hug. Nothing he said could make it better.

She had a deep abrasion on her hip; sore muscles; blue-black bruises. She bled through bandage after bandage. What hurt more was the lost opportunity. To not finish the race.

She felt confused about what happened, what she did wrong. Gwen, Patrick and Jamie watched the race replay. It was hard to see everything. Maybe there was something on the road? Or she leaned a fraction too far? No matter how hard she tried, she couldn't find a cause. Getting back on the bike without knowing a reason for the crash scared her. She tried to find a positive—she was thankful there were no broken bones, no stitches—and reminded herself the real goal was years away in Rio.

CHAPTER 23

2014 Wizard Training

Gwen and Patrick returned to the United States between the 2013 and 2014 seasons. Gwen traveled for appearances with her sponsors. She reconnected with her family. She worked on bike skills with Patrick, attacking hilly roads, mountain bike trails and cyclocross races.

On January 1, 2014, Gwen and Patrick returned to Australia and then Spain to train for a second year with Jamie and the Wollongong Wizards. In March, Gwen won a race in Australia. But then she took 12th in New Zealand.

What was she doing wrong? A crash in the Grand Final. Twelfth in New Zealand. If she moved across the world and sacrificed so much, she expected consistent results. She thought of college swimming. How she couldn't get any better. She thought of college track. How she didn't finish her last race. Had she reached her capacity in triathlon? Was it time to explore something new?

"Patrick, I'm not sure this is working. Maybe we should go home." She described her frustration, her uncertainty, her lack of confidence in this journey.

"Talk to Jamie, Gwen. I'm sure he has some ideas."

Gwen thought about it and approached him after practice.

"Take some time off," Jamie said. "Think it over. Remember, your decisions aren't sacrifices."

"What do you mean?" Gwen expected Jamie to suggest a different kind of training or outline areas to improve. Instead, he wanted her to take a step away and review her mindset. Gwen wondered if he still believed she could win at the Olympics.

"Every day you work, every day you're away from family, all the money you spend on nutrition, massage, physio, flights. Those aren't sacrifices. Those are investments."

Gwen listened.

Jamie talked about her progress. "You're doing all the little things right. If you are patient, they will add up. But it's up to you. Are you committed? Are you ready to let improved processes determine your outcomes?"

Gwen took time away to think. She and Patrick spent a few days in a French village. She didn't train. She rested and gave herself time to recharge. She asked herself questions. What was still possible? What were her options? What did she want to do?

Jamie Turner's Advice to Gwen

- Set measurable, action-driven and achievable goals.
- Make investments, not sacrifices.
- Focus on the process, not the outcome.
- Associate with people who make you better.
- Work to improve something each day.
- Instill positive habits outside of sport (change the toilet paper roll, make your bed).
- Every day, journal three achievements and three things to improve.
- Know that feelings don't have to dictate outcomes.
- Do something only when you are prepared.
- Be grateful, respectful and honest; be a good person in addition to a good athlete.

Jamie's Statement to the Press

As a coach, people choose me to assist [them] on their journey and 'steer the bus,' and I want them involved in which direction they take," he said. "They help determine their path, but they can also drive us down the wrong street. We need to learn from that, and learn how to take the right direction...I want them to eventually drive the bus with me in the passenger seat, and the ultimate goal of coaching is for them to drive the bus and me to be pretty redundant...I'll just guide and assist them. I want to empower them.

Source: Smith, Shawn. "Jamie Turner – Why He's the World's Best Triathlon Coach." January 10, 2017. Available: https://www.trizone.com.au/20170110/jamie-turner-worlds-best-triathlon-coach/.

Views from Gwen's training runs and swims in Vitoria-Gasteiz, Basque Region in Spain

Dad, Gwen, Mom in downtown Vitoria-Gasteiz

Vitoria-Gasteiz Old Quarter

CHAPTER 24

2014 Making Decisions

While in France, Gwen wrote in her journal, made lists of pros and cons and questioned herself. What was her goal? Was it to win every race or to explore her potential? Why such poor results? Was she afraid of success? Did she feel unworthy? Uncomfortable in the spotlight?

"Whatever you decide, I'm with you," Patrick said. "We'll figure it out together." Patrick said he loved her and they would team up to achieve her goals, whatever they were.

After two weeks, when Gwen returned to Spain, a swell of confidence nudged her. She remembered that winning didn't have to mean first place; winning could mean doing her best, being her best, realizing her best. She recalled how good it felt to push herself, mind and body. She remembered the thrill of competition: exercise, amplified. The satisfaction of testing herself against peers, against the world's best. I owe myself this, she thought. To see how good I can be. World Champion? Rio 2016 Olympic champion?

"I want to keep training," she said. "I'm not done. I can do more. I want to do more."

"Then I'm with you," Patrick said.

With renewed purpose, Gwen returned to daily training with the Wizards. This was her journey and she would draw the map, pinpoint her destination and chart her course.

She adopted Jamie's mantras. She found inspiration in her teammates. "Charlotte zoomed right by me on that hill today," she told Patrick. "If she does it in practice, she'll do it in a race. And I have to be able to match her." Each teammate's accomplishment challenged Gwen. Like a schoolgirl again, she used her peers as motivation.

***

Gwen's next race was in Yokohama, Japan—her favorite location for its sushi, mochi and polite and welcoming people.

Don't expect to win right away, she told herself. You have two and a half years to prepare for Rio. She recalled Jamie's advice: slow progress, one day at a time. Then, in spite of realistic expectations, she won. She loved Japan even more for this victory.

London was next—the course where she suffered a flat in the 2012 Olympics and crashed in the 2013 World Championship. As much as she loved the feeling of a win, she hated the losses more. But she refused to obsess over the past. And on her third London attempt, she won.

Don't become complacent, she thought. Every race holds a new challenge—rough waters, cobblestone streets, extreme temperatures, steep hills. Prepare for each contest. Be ready to shift attention. Expect a surprise. Anticipate an obstacle.

Next up: Chicago, USA. Only 90 minutes from where she grew up, this race presented unique pressures: hometown television journalists and newspaper reporters; a crowd filled with friends and family; life-size posters of herself; the expectation to win on home soil.

Gwen hadn't braced herself for the anxiety, the tension, the constant distractions. "Patrick, you have to help." She felt on edge with so many fans requesting photos or autographs. "Everyone recognizes me."

"What can I do?"

"I love the fans," she said. "They give me so much support."

"Spend time with each one," he said, "and I'll help wrap up the conversation."

The next time a fan asked for a selfie, Patrick gave Gwen a few minutes and then said, "Gwen, we really need to get going." She was grateful he always did what she needed.

The race started with a swim in Lake Michigan and moved to cycling on the city streets. Completing the bike leg, Gwen was 66 seconds behind. A huge deficit.

As she slipped on her running shoes, she reminded herself to stay calm. Concentrate on what's controllable. Build slowly. Keep eyes on who's ahead. There is plenty of race. Take one step at a time.

In the third of four laps, after overtaking much of the competition, Gwen approached the two leaders. Smooth cadence, she thought. Light feet. Relaxed shoulders. She ran with them for a bit, surged and overtook them both. She sprinted to the finish line and won her third WTS race of the season.

The win released built-up tension. Pleasing sponsors, finding time for family, attending to fans, sitting for photo shoots and preparing for the race. Now, with the pressure off, and a win in her home country, she felt like she could float through the rest of the day. She celebrated with family and friends. She remembered what she loved about the spotlight: motivating fans to be the best versions of themselves.

She followed up with a win in Hamburg, Germany, and for the second consecutive year, Gwen was in position to win a World Championship.

Lifesize poster in Chicago 2014

CHAPTER 25

2014 World Championship Race

Edmonton, in Alberta, Canada, hosted the 2014 World Championship race. Gwen almost quit triathlon a few months before, and now she was poised to be named the world's best. She needed to place in the top 16 to be 2014 Champion. But top 16 wasn't her goal. She aimed to win both the race and the season.

She felt confident in her string of victories. She was scared too, especially about her weakness on the bike. Swimming and cycling almost always put her behind. Running won races, but what if she got too far behind? No, she thought. Worry drains energy. She decided to zap negative thoughts.

With Gwen's and Patrick's families in the grandstand, she dove into the Edmonton lake and exited the swim in 13th place. I just need to make that front bike pack, she thought. She had a good transition, hopped on her saddle and pedaled. They're getting away. Pedal harder. But the pack took off, leaving her solo. This is not where I should be.

And then her USA teammate Sarah Haskins appeared. She was a powerhouse cyclist. "Just hang on," Sarah said. She motioned with her arm, encouraging Gwen to join the chase pack and draft off her wheel.

What is wrong? Why can't I stay with her? Gwen dropped to the tail end of the chase pack. This is a terrible position. I need to move up. She pushed and pulled her feet on the pedals, dedicating energy into each stroke, but she remained at the back. And even with Sarah at the front, the chase pack's deficit grew. From a few seconds to 30, to 45, to 60. When Gwen finished the bike leg, she was in 19th place and 78 seconds behind.

Don't panic, she thought. Just run. You have four laps to make this right. Her mind settled on breathing, stride, arms. On overtaking one competitor at a time.

At the end of lap one, her deficit had shrunk. Forty-nine seconds.

During lap two, Gwen swept past two runners, then eight more. Be patient. Steady.

At the beginning of lap three, she was 17 seconds back. Now, she could see her targets. She would pick off one at a time.

On the fourth and final lap, Gwen and two others led. They ran as a trio. Gwen remembered how hard she worked on the swim, the bike and the run to get this close to a championship. She looked for an opportunity. It was time to make a statement. To be decisive. To break away. She wondered if the others could go with her.

Gwen surged. She listened for footsteps and heard none. She accelerated and listened again. Still no footsteps. Her only target now—the finish line.

That night, Gwen Jorgensen, 2014 World Champion, celebrated with Patrick, Jamie, family, sponsors and friends. Gwen was ecstatic to be the World Champion, but she couldn't stop thinking about how tough the course was. How she struggled on the hills. How she didn't execute the way she hoped to.

With Elizabeth and a friend

The race mirrored her 2014 training when poor results and doubt almost ended her season. But in both the season and the race, she corrected weaknesses. Emphasized strengths. Kept her thoughts positive. Looked ahead. Surrounded herself with talented people. Controlled the controllables. Made her investments pay.

Signing autographs

Edmonton podium celebration

Gwen and Patrick's Wedding

A few months before Gwen won the 2014 World Championship in Edmonton, she and Patrick designed, printed and mailed wedding invitations. After the World Championship race, Patrick bought a blue suit and Gwen bought a long white dress.

When: Saturday, October 4, 2014

Where: Rivers Eatery (a wood-fired pizza restaurant in Cable, Wisconsin)

Who: 150 of Patrick's and Gwen's family and friends

We said we didn't need any decorations; however, friends turned Rivers Eatery into absolute perfection. A local farmer saw our party tent in the back of the restaurant and asked what was going on. When he heard it was a wedding, he hopped in his car, drove to his farm and picked up hay bales and pumpkins to decorate (it's an amazing group of people in Cable, WI, and that's a big reason why it's our favorite place to vacation). Other friends (Trudi Rebsamen, Dennis Kruse, Tom Schuler, and Deb Wood) even went so far as to press beautiful fall leaves for table decor!

I wish I could describe the atmosphere when we walked up to the altar. The room literally roared with love and support. It was the most exhilarating and happiest moment of my life. No WTS win, Olympics, or other event could ever or will ever compare. I couldn't have been happier with the night. Molly and the Danger Band played live music throughout the night and we left a little after 1 a.m. It was perfection.

Source: http://www.gwenjorgensen.com/blog/wedding-bliss

CHAPTER 26

2015-2016 Rio Qualification

Gwen looked at the 2014 World Champion trophy. It reminded her she was the best triathlete in the world. That she broke records. Eight World Triathlon Series gold medals. Five consecutive World Triathlon Series wins. In a few years, she had risen from a CPA to World Champion triathlete. Sometimes, it seemed like a dream and she almost couldn't believe it.

Success in 2014 strengthened and encouraged her. But Rio 2016 held the ultimate prize: Olympic gold. To get there, she needed to qualify for the USA Olympic team. That became her priority.

Gwen had spent months improving her swim. Now, she concentrated on biking and the fear that often handicapped her: fear of speed, fear of downhills, fear of riding so close, so fast. She worked with Patrick and Jamie to find solutions.

"Gwen, I found a race car track," Patrick said. "And a driver to show you speed."

"How does that help?" she said. "I ride a bike, not a car."

Jamie explained. "You need to be confident on the bike. If you can tolerate car velocity, your body and brain will tolerate bike speed more easily." Jamie repeated his theory often: "Get comfortable with the uncomfortable."

At the race track, Gwen rode shotgun at 100 miles per hour as the driver careened around curves. The engine roared. Her throat felt dry. On every turn, momentum yanked her body and her heart rate rocketed.

"Wanna give it a go?" the driver said.

"This is scary enough."

During the session, she acclimated a bit to the speed. Fast turns frightened her less. Her hands stopped sweating. Her stomach no longer convulsed.

The next day, she and Patrick rode their bikes. When they rode fast, she felt less intimidated, more in control.

A few months later, Patrick worked with Gwen's sponsor Red Bull to find additional cycling support and coaching. "We found this motorcycle driver who will take you down a mountain."

"What?" she said.

"Then, you'll go back up and do it again on your bike. It's just like the race track. If you're used to fast descents on a motorcycle, downhill cycling will seem easier."

The thought of plunging down a mountain made her feel faint and fragile, like a teacup balanced on her great-grandma's knee. But she trusted Jamie and Patrick to help solve problems. The race car experience alleviated fear—she hoped the motorcycle would too.

Gwen hugged the driver from behind as he roared down the mountain, leaning into turns, gauging speed versus safety. On the motorcycle, her pulse raced, her mind edgy and skittish, but when she got on her bicycle, speed seemed easier to control. Her head quieted. She trusted herself and the bicycle more. And Patrick was right, the bike felt slower.

Gwen entered the 2015 triathlon season the favorite, expected to repeat as World Champion. The expectation added stress. Reporters asked if she could win six in a row, or seven, or eight. For each reporter, she had the same answer: "I take it one race at a time." She hadn't lost a race in ten months. She loved the wins, but another race always loomed where she had to prove herself again.

Gwen dominated 2015's first races. She won in Abu Dhabi, Auckland, Gold Coast, Yokohama, London and Hamburg. The wins bolstered her confidence as she targeted the 2015 Rio test event. Held in August on the Olympic course, only two USA athletes could qualify there for the 2016 Games. Qualification was vital to reaching her goal.

On Sunday, August 2, 70 women lined up on Rio de Janeiro's Copacabana Beach. Gwen put one foot forward and leaned. She waited for the start. Suddenly, women on her right sprinted. What? Did the horn sound? She dashed to the water. Apparently, no one on her left heard the horn either because they also started late. Officials didn't call a false start, so the race went on.

In the water, arms and elbows jabbed. Feet whacked. Someone belted Gwen in the face. Is my tooth chipped? Don't think about it. Be present.

Gwen exited in 19th place, but a fast transition put her with the first bike pack. Gwen remained there and dismounted with the top three. In transition, she wrestled with her bike. Why was the wheel not spinning? It felt loose, so she picked up the bike, hoisted it in the air and ran with it to her rack. No time to analyze a wheel malfunction. Doesn't matter. Get off the helmet, get on the shoes and glasses and run.

Gwen and two USA teammates formed a front run pack with a pair of British women. After two laps, Gwen dashed ahead and one of the Brits went with her. They ran together for a lap, but the pace felt slow. Gwen accelerated again and ran solo to the finish line. The win secured her place at the Olympic Games.

It felt like releasing the pressure on a can of bubbly water. She popped the top with this win and stress about qualifying fizzed away. Now she could concentrate on Rio 2016. One more year to hone her swim. One more year to polish her cycling. One more year to perfect her run.

That night, Gwen, Patrick and Jamie celebrated with a party for 100. They reserved a room in a restaurant where fairy lights decorated a balcony. Gwen's sponsor Red Bull paid for the evening. For several hours, waiters served elegant appetizers and exotic drinks. Gwen wandered among guests, thanking sponsors, family and fans for their support. She achieved her goal of qualification and celebrated this success. But the work didn't stop—still so much to do. She left as early as possible because the next day she had a training session and a photo shoot.

Copacabana Beach where the race started

***

One race remained in the WTS season—the World Championship. On September 18 in Chicago, Gwen vied for her second world title. She dove into Lake Michigan with 75 women. Sixth to mount her bike, she stayed in the lead pack. Toward the end of the run, she established distance between herself and the others, won the race and was named 2015 World Champion. She now had two World Championships and 15 consecutive World Triathlon Series wins. Her confidence grew.

But with each win, conjecture appeared. She tried to ignore triathlon blogs where writers discussed her domination. Where they wondered if her hot streak could continue—if she could remain undefeated through the Olympics.

Triathlon outlets wanted interviews. Her hometown Wisconsin paper asked for a statement. Magazines in Minnesota requested photos. She was now the winningest woman in the history of the sport, so international outlets pursued her too. Gwen consented to several interviews and declined others. She prioritized training and preparation for her singular goal: Olympic gold.

After her second World Championship win, Gwen and Patrick took a two-month break in Minnesota. They traveled for sponsor appearances and spent a few days with family. On January 1, 2016, they returned to Australia and then Spain to train for August 20, 2016—the Rio Olympic triathlon.

In her first events of the season, Gwen won a Continental Cup and a World Cup.

Her first World Triathlon Series race was in Gold Coast, Australia. "I'm like a target," she said to Patrick. "Everyone is aiming for me."

Competitors talked openly about attempting to defeat Gwen Jorgensen. They revealed their strategy to distance her from strong swimmers, to tire her on the bike, to out-think her. To work together to beat her.

NBC Olympics posted an article about Gwen's competitors. They quoted athletes and concluded with an analysis.

"There will be times where we are in a bike pack, and you realize that some people are like, 'Gwen's here, let's give up,'" said fellow U.S. triathlete Sarah True. "I'm like, 'Keep on racing! Always keep on racing!'"

"You know she can't be touched on the run," True said. "You have to open up a gap in the swim and the bike."

...To defeat Jorgensen, in the absence of any bike accidents or malfunctions, a competitor will likely have to make a very aggressive move on the bicycle leg, and then have enough endurance to maintain the lead on the run leg.

Source: Rubinroit, Seth. "Who Can Beat Gwen Jorgensen?" *NBC Olympics.* August 19, 2016. Available: http://archivepyc.nbcolympics.com/news/who-can-beat-gwen-jorgensen.

Gwen tried to ignore the media chatter. She homed in on the Gold Coast event.

After a swim in the Gold Coast, Australia, waters and a transition to the bike leg, three riders broke away. Gwen fell behind; she failed to catch them on the run. It was her first loss in two years.

A few hours after the race, Gwen replied to a family email. Her parents thought she looked exhausted on video coverage.

when I sprint I get tired. :)
wish I was more upset about the race, but no tears from me
I was super tired on that bike and just wasn't as good as the others today.
I did fight for 2nd tho so that's good
we head to Wollongong until Yoko then to Spain after Yoko
gwen

Gwen reflected on the race. If she wanted to win at the Olympics, she had to stay in the front of the bike pack. She couldn't let a breakaway leave her behind. Although the loss stung, as each one did, she used it to correct mistakes. Then, she concentrated on her end-goal.

Analyzing Gwen's loss, former Olympic triathlete Emma Snowsill said, "I honestly think, as scary as this sounds, it can be a blessing in disguise for Gwen... it can [take]...that pressure off for her."

***

In the next two WTS events, Gwen returned to winning. She took first in Yokohama, Japan, and Leeds, Great Britain. Then in Hamburg, Germany, her final race before the Olympics, she missed the front bike pack and couldn't make up time on the run. She finished third and analysts shouted doubt. *Is this the chink in Gwen's armor? What will happen if there is a breakaway in Rio?*

Gwen reminded herself that Gold Coast and Hamburg didn't matter. Only Rio mattered. I have to learn from this. Find the lesson. Apply it to training. The goal is still the same. To be ready in one month, on August 20, to combine the best of what I know, with the best I can be. In Rio.

Gwen Dominated World Triathlon Series in 2014, 2015 and 2016

- 1st - ITU World Cup Mooloolaba, Australia (March 15, 2014)
- 12th - ITU WTS Auckland, New Zealand (April 6, 2014)
- 3rd - ITU WTS Cape Town, South Africa (April 26, 2014)
- 1st - ITU WTS Yokohama, Japan (May 17, 2014)
- 1st - ITU WTS London, UK (May 31, 2014)
- 1st - ITU WTS Chicago, USA (June 28, 2014)
- 1st - ITU WTS Hamburg, Germany (July 12, 2014)
- 1st - British Sprint Champs Liverpool, UK (August 10, 2014)
- 1st - ITU WTS Grand Final, Edmonton, Canada (September 1, 2014)
- 1st - ITU WTS Abu Dhabi, United Arab Emirates (March 6, 2015)
- 1st - ITU WTS Auckland, New Zealand (March 29, 2015)
- 1st - ITU WTS Gold Coast, Australia (April 11, 2015)
- 1st - ITU WTS Yokohama, Japan (May 16, 2015)
- 1st - ITU WTS London, UK (May 31, 2015)
- 1st - ITU WTS Hamburg, Germany (July 18, 2015)
- 1st - Test Event and USA Olympic Trials Rio de Janeiro, Brazil (August 2, 2015)
- 1st - ITU WTS Grand Final Chicago, USA (September 18, 2015)
- 1st - ITU Continental Cup Wollongong, Australia (March 5, 2016)
- 1st - ITU World Cup New Plymouth, New Zealand (April 3, 2016)
- 2nd - ITU WTS Gold Coast, Australia (April 9, 2016)
- 1st - ITU WTS Yokohama, Japan (May 14, 2016)
- 1st - ITU WTS Leeds, Great Britain (June 12, 2016)
- 3rd - ITU WTS Hamburg, Germany (July 16, 2016)
- 1st - ITU WTS Hamburg, Germany Mixed Team Relay World Championship (July 17, 2016)

Gwen: The Winningest Woman in Triathlon's History

- 25 gold medals
- 37 podium finishes
- First USA woman to win a World Triathlon Series race
- 12-race WTS winning streak
- 17 ITU World Triathlon Series wins
- The only woman to win a world title after a perfect undefeated WTS season
- 2013 and 2014 USA Triathlon Triathlete of the Year
- 2014 and 2015 USA Elite National Champion
- 2014 and 2015 WTS World Champion
- 2016 WTS Mixed Team Relay World Champion

Gwen Tuned Out Social Media

Naysayers and doubters posted on social media. Sometimes, comments stung and created self-doubt. Gwen talked to Patrick about what she saw online and he gave her this advice:
- accept that everyone has differing opinions;
- recognize that outsiders don't know you or your process or goals;
- know what people post online is not what they'd say in person;
- don't ruminate on what you read;
- be confident and outside opinions will matter less;
- trust those closest to you; they know your work best;
- talk about your anxiety or distress; it will help you feel better; and
- remember, your emotions don't dictate your outcomes.

Gwen Jorgensen Scholarship Fund

To inspire junior triathletes to reach their potential and achieve their dreams, Gwen started a scholarship fund.

The Gwen Jorgensen Scholarship was awarded annually from 2014 through 2017. Recipients used the funds for programming, training or travel. In addition to money, Gwen provided a year of mentoring to each scholarship winner.

Gwen and Patrick contributed their own money and then other organizations and corporations, like ROKA and USA Triathlon Foundation, also contributed. In total, more than $60,000 was given to youth triathletes.

Gwen said, "I encouraged the athletes to contact me whenever they needed anything or had a question. My favorite part...was receiving text message updates about how they raced or questions about both racing and life. I don't have all the answers, but I love being a part of their triathlon journey."

Source: https://www.teamusa.org/USA-Triathlon/News/Articles-and-Releases /2016/June/28/US-Olympian-Gwen-Jorgensen-to-Award-Scholarships-to-Junior-Triathletes.

CHAPTER 27

Rio 2016: Two Days Before the Olympic Triathlon

> "I've said for four years that this was my goal. I wanted to cross that line and get the gold medal."
>
> —Gwen Jorgensen

Leading up to the Olympic Games, experts called Gwen the favorite. She had been undefeated for two years and won 17 World Triathlon Series races. She was the 2014 and 2015 World Champion.

Since her string of victories snapped in Australia and Germany, experts saw weakness. They questioned her ability to win Olympic gold. Could a breakaway ruin her race? Would her running be enough to recover from a deficit? Could she defeat the defending Olympic champion, Switzerland's Nicola Spirig? What about the women who defeated her in Gold Coast and Hamburg? For Gwen, past races were only steps to her real goal: Olympic gold. But reporters were in Rio, eager for interviews.

"Gwen, there's a media conference tomorrow," Patrick said. "I think you should go."

Gwen preferred to center on her race, but she knew fans should see and hear from her. "I know. What's planned?"

"It's a round table," Patrick said. "Reporters sit at stations and you spend ten minutes with someone and then go to the next."

"How long?"

"An hour, max."

Gwen agreed and fielded questions—*What is your race plan? Do you think you can defeat the defending Olympic champion? Are you nervous about Zika virus in the water?* She responded as honestly as she could—*I'm ready for any scenario. I can only control my own race. Officials say the water meets safety standards*—and left after exactly 60 minutes.

Later that day, Gwen's family landed in Rio. Her mom, dad, Elizabeth and Elizabeth's boyfriend, Josh, stayed at a hotel a few blocks away. As soon as they arrived, they walked to Gwen's room with packages for Gwen's coach, Jamie. Her sponsor ASICS had sent hats and shirts for him. It was against Olympic rules for athletes to wear unauthorized clothing, but coaches and family could wear a sponsor's logo. ASICS wanted their brand visible.

"Thanks, Mom." Gwen hugged her, grabbed the packages and tossed them on the bed. "Thanks, Dad." She hugged him and Elizabeth and Josh too.

A bright orange frame leaned against a wall. "Cool bike," her dad said.

"Specialized designed it. Just for this race." Her bike sponsor made the special edition for their Olympic triathletes.

"Touch it," Patrick said.

Gwen's dad looked at her as if asking permission.

"Go ahead. It changes color."

He gripped the orange frame and took his hand away. Where his fingers were, the bike was now yellow. He dug his phone out of his pocket. "I gotta have a picture for everybody at home. Does this help your race?"

"Nope. It's just for fun."

"You have other jobs for us?" her mom said.

Gwen counted on family for help with errands. She was thankful they didn't talk about the race and didn't expect too much of her time. "I need a can of yellow Red Bull."

For the cycling portion of the race, Gwen pre-set bottles on her bike frame. She filled them with half water, half Red Bull. The Red Bull supplied carbohydrates, caffeine, sodium and taurine. Diluting it with water made the solution gentler on her stomach. "Could you pick one up at the Red Bull House?"

Red Bull and other companies hosted hospitality houses where athletes and their families ate, relaxed and watched the Games. Gwen chose not to use them pre-race but suggested her family should.

Patrick's family also arrived in Rio and helped with her preparation. Gwen appreciated their efforts because it meant she could concentrate on her race. The race where, in two days, she hoped to prove she was the best in the world.

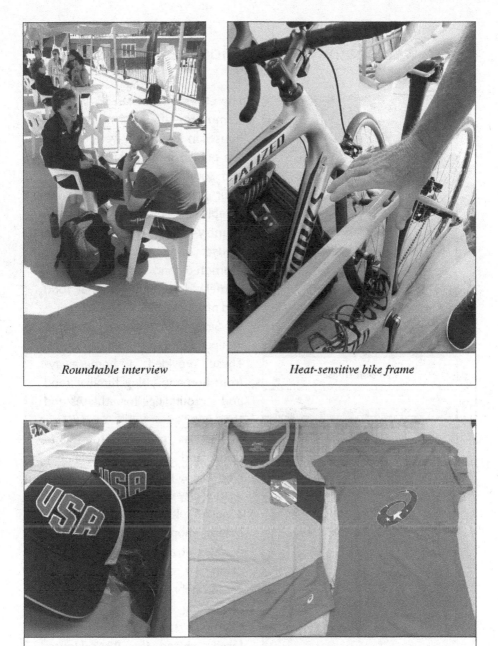

Roundtable interview

Heat-sensitive bike frame

ASICS apparel for family and coach

Gwen's Family Visited Hospitality Houses

Red Bull House

Cans of Red Bull requested by Gwen

There were more than 35 Olympic Committee-affiliated hospitality houses in Rio. Some were open to the public, some required a ticket and some were for athletes and their families only. Many were established by a participating country—Italy House, British House and Austria House promoted and advertised their homeland through national food and products.

Several companies created independent hospitality houses. These provided a home-away-from-home, offering familiar food and surroundings for athletes and their families.

Houses provided food and drink and screens playing live Olympic action. Some resembled a small city where guests could get a haircut, play video games, eat ice cream, shop for Olympic apparel or relax at an outdoor cafe. Most offered a space where athletes could celebrate after competition.

During their five-day Rio Olympics stay, Gwen and Patrick's family visited the P&G House, Oakley House, Red Bull House and USA House.

CHAPTER 28

Rio 2016: One Day Before the Olympic Triathlon

> "The week of the race, I had never been so calm. I wasn't nervous, but instead, I was excited."
>
> —Gwen Jorgensen

On August 19, 2016, Gwen woke early, as usual. One more day. Tomorrow, there would be a new Olympic champion in women's triathlon.

For four years, Gwen's coach taught her to concentrate on the processes. Wishing or hoping for Olympic gold wouldn't make it happen. The key was in the process of swimming: enter the water at full speed, keep head down on the first few strokes, raise elbows in the water. The process of biking: be aggressive, look up the road, keep weight on the outside foot when turning. The process of running: relax shoulders, swing arms, build throughout the run.

Gwen didn't wish for Olympic gold. She didn't worry about the weather. She didn't stress over another athlete's race plan. Instead, she reviewed each discipline. She anticipated any scenario. She prepared to be spontaneous and ready to react. She kept her mind on what she could control.

Her coach's second lesson: consistency. Slow progress, one day at a time. Get better each day. Make each day's work add up. So, on the day before the Olympic race, Gwen did what she always did. She swam, biked and ran.

Then, she made one final request to the chef. "Could we have a rice dish tonight, please? Chicken for protein and lots of greens? Maybe broccoli or asparagus? And a large salad with boiled eggs and spinach?"

"No problem, Gwen. It's been a pleasure working with you."

"Thank you so much. And my race is tomorrow. Can we have oats in the morning? With nuts and dried fruit?"

"See me when you come down." He gave her a smile. "And I'll poach an egg for you too."

As they left, Patrick handed the chef an envelope, a gift for accommodating their requests.

*Gwen's workouts the day before her
2016 Olympic race*

*Gwen's process goals for the 2016
Olympic triathlon race*

At dinner, Gwen ate the chef's specially prepared meal. She drank lots of bottled water. She enjoyed one square of dark chocolate.

She returned to her room and elevated her feet. Before bedtime, she documented the day in her journal.

Then, she turned to the page for August 20, 2016. This was where she had written reminders for the Rio 2016 Olympic triathlon.

A sense of calm coursed through her. Of readiness. Of anticipation and excitement. Her work was complete. She only needed to repeat in the race what she did every day in practice.

She got in bed at 8:30. She turned off the television. Dimmed the lights. And slept.

Gwen's Journal

Many athletes keep a journal to record thoughts and goals. It allows them to see progress and is later a keepsake. Some coaches require athletes to keep a journal. They may give instructions for what to enter, questions to answer or statistics to record. Writing may clear the mind; once a thought is written, the athlete can concentrate on other matters.

Gwen's journal held her accountable; if she wrote something down, she was more likely to follow through. In her journal, Gwen wrote three things she did well and three things she could improve. She also
- set goals,
- reflected on progress,
- jotted ideas,
- made plans,
- recorded results,
- acknowledged failures,
- celebrated efforts and success,
- asked questions and
- noted hopes and dreams.

Gwen's Poached Egg Recipe

While in Rio, Gwen requested the chef make some of her favorite foods. She often ate poached eggs on top of her morning oats.

INGREDIENTS
1-3 eggs
1 tablespoon vinegar

DIRECTIONS
1. Bring a medium-sized pot of water to a boil.
2. Once boiling, add 1 tablespoon white vinegar.
3. Crack eggs onto a plate.
4. When the eggs are on the plate, ensure there is a membrane surrounding the yolk and the egg whites.
5. Whisk the boiling water. (Be careful.)
6. Once the water is swirling, drop in the eggs.
7. The poaching process will take 2-3 minutes.
8. Remove each egg individually with a slotted spoon. Place onto a plate lined with a paper towel. This removes excess liquid.
9. Serve immediately

Gwen's poached egg on oats

Gwen's poached eggs on top of a sweet potato

Gwen Learned to Fuel Her Body

Gwen learned about nutrition from her coaches, nutritionists, teammates and mentors. In high school, her swim coach recommended she keep a food journal for a week. Gwen wrote down everything. Her coach reviewed her entries and advised her to consume more protein and keep eating fresh fruits and vegetables.

During college and her professional career, Gwen met with nutritionists. They taught her to eat calorie-dense meals before a hard workout or competition; fuel before, during and after workouts; and eat consistently. From experience, Gwen found her body performed best with oats in the morning; rice, protein and veggies midday; and potato and salad in the evening.

Gwen and Patrick searched out food experts to teach them about nutrition and preparation. Alan Murchison, a Michelin star chef, coached Patrick in purchasing and preparing fresh meat and fish, and Gwen partnered with Skratch Labs, a nutrition supplement company, to design fuel for before, during and after her workout.

Gwen and Patrick treated food as fuel, but also as something to enjoy. They explored new foods like tortilla de patatas, blood sausage or steak tartare. And when Gwen got a sweet craving, she satisfied it with ice cream or one square of dark chocolate.

CHAPTER 29

Rio 2016: Olympic Triathlon Race Day

"It's not every four years. It's every day."
—Gwen Jorgensen

Gwen woke to an alarm and checked her phone. So many messages. More in email and on Facebook and Twitter. She felt grateful for everyone's support and proud to represent them—her mom, dad, Elizabeth and Patrick; Jamie; teammates; fans; sponsors; USAT; her country. She felt responsible too—for a win.

Race day had a routine. Habit became critical. Familiarity built confidence. So, Gwen began, like she did every day, with a bottle of water. As she dressed, she said to Patrick, "Can you bring me some food?" He would pick up a bowl of oats and fruit from the chef.

"Just thinking that," he said and grabbed his room key. "Usual toppings?"

"Lots of berries." She pulled on a sweatshirt. "And remind Adam about my poached egg."

"Coffee?" He leaned in and kissed her.

"Small one."

After she ate her breakfast, Gwen surveyed her gear, checking it against a list. She packed last-minute items like earbuds and chargers.

In the bathroom, she moistened her required temporary tattoos. Peeling the numbers from wet plastic, she aligned them on her arm and pressed. She worked until both arms and legs wore the number 20. She applied similar stickers to her helmet and bike.

Equipment ready, Gwen and Patrick hefted bags to their backs. Patrick carried an extra wheel. Gwen guided her bike by the saddle. They exited the hotel and crossed the street to Copacabana Beach where Gwen entered the athlete tent. "Checking in please," she said. "Gwen Jorgensen."

An official handed her an information sheet and inspected her equipment. He measured her wheels and her bike's height. He looked for illegal motorized assistance. He verified the logo size on her swimsuits. He inspected her goggles and sunglasses. The process took longer than any other Gwen had experienced. Even in London 2012, the equipment check was quicker. Apparently, each Olympic experience was unique.

After her equipment was approved, Gwen located her assigned number 20 bike rack in the blue-carpeted transition zone. Her name and number marked the rack and equipment box. She double-checked again: swim goggles and cap, helmet, sunglasses, water bottle, bike shoes, elastic bands for aligning shoes on the bike, running shoes. How was her tire pressure? Were her brakes working? She pressed on the tires with her thumb and spun the wheels.

Then, she began her physical preparation. She ran strides on the roads. She stretched bands. She returned to the athlete tent and biked 15 minutes on a trainer. She did mobility drills for core and arms. She mentally checked off each warm-up.

Her coach, Jamie, chatted with Patrick a few yards away. There if she needed him. But she knew he wouldn't say much. The work was done. She just needed to repeat what she knew she could do.

"Gwen." Patrick laid his arm on her shoulder. He kissed her. "You need anything before I go?"

She shook her head, kissed him back and watched him leave. She saw him wave and call to Elizabeth, who happened to be walking by. Gwen knew Elizabeth, family and friends felt nervous. They remembered the London Olympic race when Gwen got a flat tire; they thought about the wind and heat; they worried about all the things that could go wrong.

CHAPTER 30

Rio 2016: Olympic Triathlon Start Line

"Four years ago, I set a goal: to win the Rio Olympics."
—Gwen Jorgensen

The clock registered minutes until the 11 a.m. start. On Gwen's ankles, she had timing chips. She wore her blue trisuit with stars and stripes on the side and "USA Jorgensen" on the front.

Gwen and the other women gathered on the beach. Athletes shuffled feet, swung arms, tugged swim caps and adjusted goggles. They prepared their bodies, minds and emotions as they waited to start the race.

Spectators filled the grandstand seats. Gwen's family and friends, 17 of them, sat together. Her mom, dad, Elizabeth, Josh and uncles; Pat's mom, dad and sister, Paige; high school friends; college friends; her agent; and sponsor representatives. Everyone dressed in red, white and blue. They brought water bottles, video cameras and USA flags. Fans from around the world sat nearby, wearing their own countries' colors. An overflow crowd stood in the roped-off beach area.

There was an NBC broadcast on television. A computer live stream. Updates on Twitter and Facebook. Millions watched.

Announcers spoke in Portuguese and English. They called each athlete's name. One by one, 55 women from 31 countries jogged toward the start line.

When all were lined up, music played from the speakers, suspenseful, like the underscore to a movie. The crowd hushed. Temperatures reached close to 80°. The air smelled like sea and sunscreen. Winds at 17 miles per hour rippled the ocean. Then, silence as the women waited, one foot forward, ready to sprint.

Gwen's family, friends and sponsors in the grandstands   *Beach line up (Gwen on right)*

Gwen's Timing Chip

In most professional triathlons, athletes wore small, lightweight chips. They were often attached to the ankles with straps and identified the athlete as they crossed electronic mats on the course.

Gwen's chips recorded her time for the swim leg and each lap of the bike and run. These electronically recorded splits allowed fans to track the event as it happened.

CHAPTER 31

Rio 2016: Olympic Triathlon Swim

"I knew there was only one thing I could control: my own race."

—Gwen Jorgensen

The horn blasted and 55 athletes dashed to the water, knees high as they pushed through waves. Then, they dolphin-dived into freestyle. Stroke by stroke, they advanced into the ocean, growing so small the crowd on Copacabana Beach would no longer be able to identify them.

At the first buoy, they formed a single pack led by a Spanish athlete. Two swam behind the Spaniard, then the rest of the pack, four-wide. Gwen positioned herself toward the front, one of the first ten.

For 20 minutes, the women fought ocean current, battled competitors' arms and legs and contested personal limits. Gwen ran through her goals. Be alert, aware, intent, assertive. Enjoy suffering. Keep elbows high. Sight the markers. Maximize the draft from those in front. She stayed with the top ten.

With 200 meters to go, Gwen jostled for position. With so many arms, legs and bodies, she didn't know what happened. Swimmers moved ahead and she exited the water behind a couple dozen others.

She had trained herself to look forward, not back. To banish thoughts about place. To resist analyzing how she got behind. To only concentrate on what comes next.

Running up the beach to the transition zone, she ripped off her goggles and cap. Her body felt heavy. Her legs burned. When she got to her bike rack, she tossed her cap and goggles in the bin—made sure they didn't bounce out. Pulled on her helmet. Her pulse raged. She allowed muscle memory from a million drills to control her fingers as she fastened the straps. She was 11 seconds behind the leader. She lifted her bike from the rack. Running barefoot, steering the bike under one hand, she crossed the line and mounted her saddle. She pedaled as hard as she could to stay in the front bike pack where she rode at the back. It's now or never, she lectured herself. Push, push, push. Stay with the leaders this first lap—it might be the hardest thing you ever do, but it's make it or break it.

How Gwen Mounted and Dismounted a Bike

Professional triathletes mount and dismount barefoot before or after the designated lines. There is a penalty for mounting or dismounting at the wrong place.

To mount:

1. Before the triathlon, Gwen clipped her shoes to the pedals and held them temporarily upright with rubber bands.
2. During transition, while running, she held the saddle with her right hand and guided the bike to the mount line.
3. After crossing the mount line, she grabbed her handlebars with both hands, pushed off with her left foot and swung her right leg over the saddle.
4. She pedaled on top of her pre-attached shoes. (Rubber bands automatically snapped.)
5. When there was time and space, she inserted her feet and tightened her shoes.

To dismount:

1. At the end of the bike leg, Gwen slid her feet out of her shoes. She continued pedaling on top of her shoes.
2. Approaching the dismount line, she swung her right leg over the rear wheel and brought it between the bike and her left leg.
3. She stepped off the pedal, landed on her right foot and began running.
4. She let go of the handlebars and continued running while guiding the bike by the saddle.

CHAPTER 32

Rio 2016: Olympic Triathlon Bike

"I know when the big race comes, practicing under fatigue and pressure will have been good preparation."

—Gwen Jorgensen

The 40-kilometer (approximately 25-mile) bike leg would take over an hour. It was often Gwen's biggest challenge, but she spent years preparing. She almost conquered her fear of speed and descent. She built miles of riding, developing leg muscles. She learned to shift and balance and brake; to quickly change a wheel; to unclip her shoes; to mount and dismount; to lean on fast turns; to read a bike pack. Today, she focused on staying with the leaders.

Gwen knew the best cyclists in the race. Most she faced many times: Bermuda's Flora Duffy; New Zealand's Andrea Hewitt; Great Britain's Vicky Holland and Non Stanford. All stood on the podium frequently. But the reigning Olympic champion, Switzerland's Nicola Spirig, avoided much of the WTS race season. Media reported Nicola and her coach played mind games—they wanted to surprise Gwen in Rio. When reporters had asked about Nicola, Gwen said, "I can only control the controllables. I'm concentrating on my own race."

At the start of the bike leg, Flora led the front pack of 30. On the inclines, Gwen stood on her pedals and moved ahead. On the downhills, she lost time. Despite her work on descents, she still rode conservatively.

The fast pace, combined with grueling uphills, demanded strength and endurance. As the pack accelerated, eight riders dropped off. Gwen monitored the group but concentrated on her own execution: when to shift, how to lean, where to place herself. Be present, she told herself. You worked four years for this. Stay in every moment.

Vicky, Non, Nicola and Andrea took turns at the front. Gwen wanted to be closer. At any point, one of them could break away.

When Nicola led, two more cyclists dropped from the pack. Gwen moved to the middle. Occasionally, she made her way to the front.

A video cameraman, perched backward on a motorcycle, monitored the leaders. His footage appeared around the world and on the giant screen where Gwen's family and friends watched. Gwen reached for her water bottle, drank a few pulls, glanced at Nicola and smiled. Gwen felt strong and confident. Despite the physical demands and mental challenges, she enjoyed this race more than any other. The pack shrank as more riders fell off.

Flora rotated the lead with Nicola, Andrea and Non. A few times, Gwen took a turn too. She felt powerful, in control, ready to respond. It was one of the few races that felt like play.

Nicola returned to the front and the speed increased. Experts considered her the strongest cyclist. As reigning Olympic champion, she had experience with high-stakes competitions and knew how to win. She would want to tire her competition. She led them across the road. The pack followed, single file. Nicola circled one arm, indicating another should take the front. Gwen remained in second, with the rest behind. Be patient, Gwen told herself. Stay where you are. The others must have thought the same because no one relieved Nicola.

On the eighth and final lap, 18 riders from 13 nations remained in the front pack. They battled each other—the world's best from Switzerland, Bermuda, Great Britain, New Zealand, Australia, the United States, the Netherlands, Sweden, Chile, Japan, Italy, Mexico and South Africa. On the final descent, approaching transition, Gwen led.

In the last few meters, everyone loosened their shoes and slid out their feet. They pedaled barefoot, on top of their shoes, toward the transition zone. Each swung one leg over her saddle and coasted. Concentrate on the dismount, she thought. The ride isn't over yet.

At the dismount line, Gwen hopped off and ran barefoot, bike under one hand. She pivoted her thoughts to transition. No time for a penalty: rack the bike legally; get everything in the box. Make it quick: clean release of the helmet latch; shoes on fast; speedy steps out of the zone. She executed each move and felt relief. The biggest challenges were over. Now, she could run—her formula for a win. But she never competed on foot against Nicola. No matter, she thought. I have my own race to run.

Gwen Drafted on the Bike

In draft legal races, cyclists can use another rider's momentum to their benefit. Cyclists alternate turns at the front where the work is harder. By sharing the lead, each rider is able to do more than she could solo. The success of drafting varies, based on the size of the pack and rider position.

When Gwen drafted, the rider ahead blocked the wind and Gwen expended less energy. It took time and practice to learn how near to follow and where to sit in the group. Before Gwen learned to draft and share the lead, competitors were sometimes angry she didn't do her fair share at the front. But in Rio, Gwen knew how to share the lead; keeping Nicola at the front of the pack was tactical; she hoped to tire her.

CHAPTER 33

Rio 2016: Olympic Triathlon Run

"I can tell you that there is no playbook for triathlon and what happened on August 20th has never happened before and will likely never happen again."

—Gwen Jorgensen

A few minutes out of transition from bike to run, Gwen and Nicola approached a water station. They had established a gap between themselves and the rest of the field. At the hydration station were wet sponges and water bottles. Gwen doused her head, trying to combat bright sun and the 81% humidity that made Rio a tropical oven.

Gwen led, breaking the wind, with Nicola tucked behind. Gwen concentrated on run technique. She brought down her shoulders and relaxed her arms. She eliminated extra movement that could sap energy. She stayed level as she glided across the pavement.

On the second of four laps, Gwen, in her blue shoes and stars-and-stripes suit, still ran in front. Nicola, in her white shoes and red Switzerland suit, stayed close.

Gwen planned to build throughout the 10-kilometer run. She wanted to surge in the second or third lap and drop any competition. But Nicola was still with her. Was Nicola getting tired? Gwen wanted to know. She let Nicola lead so she could get a look. How was her stride? Were her shoulders tight? Was her breathing labored? Gwen would watch and wait for a chance to accelerate.

Experts said the World Champion in any sport often could not repeat that success at the Olympics. Would this be true for Gwen, the 2014 and 2015 World Champion? She banished those thoughts.

Nicola, now leading, darted across the road and Gwen followed. The pace slowed. Nicola motioned for Gwen to take over. "Let's share the lead," Nicola said.

"I led the last two laps," Gwen said.

"I already have a medal."

"I don't care." Gwen smiled. "You also are a mother and that's more impressive!"

Nicola gestured for Gwen to lead. Gwen shook her head. For a full minute, they conversed. Fans shouted, "Just run!"

This conversation felt strange to Gwen. Competitors never talked for so long during the run. Was Nicola trying to throw Gwen off? Was she using conversation to disrupt Gwen's rhythm?

Beginning the fourth and final lap, Nicola led with Gwen tucked behind.

Entering a tailwind, Gwen saw an opportunity. If she sped up now, maybe she could create distance. How would Nicola respond? She wasn't sure, but she reminded herself, I can only control my own race.

Gwen increased her speed and burst ahead. It felt good to be decisive. To make a statement about her intent. The street crowd was so loud, she couldn't tell if Nicola was with her. She didn't look back. She didn't worry about Nicola's position. She eyed the road ahead.

After almost two hours, she had five more minutes to get to the finish line ahead of 55 other athletes—including the defending Olympic champion Nicola Spirig.

CHAPTER 34

Rio 2016: Olympic Triathlon End of Run

"I couldn't hear Nicola behind me...The crowds were too loud."

—Gwen Jorgensen

Race conditions were perfect. No cold water to induce hypothermia. No extreme temperatures to spawn heat stroke. No rain to create slick spots. Gwen survived the bike leg without a flat or crash. She and Nicola led throughout the run and within minutes, the 2016 Olympic champion would be crowned.

The motorcycle roared ahead with the cameraman on the back, his lens on Gwen as she focused on the road, feet in rhythm, powering toward the finish.

Gwen approached the capacity grandstand crowd. But how close was Nicola? Was she within striking distance? If Gwen tired, could Nicola surge and overtake her?

On the blue carpet, Gwen did not slow down to grab an American flag. She did not wave to fans. She sprinted, arms driving, knees lifting.

With only a few more steps, Gwen looked over her shoulder. She saw no one. She advanced several more steps and checked again. No one. The realization hit.

She would be the Olympic champion.

Four years of training in the water, on the bike, in her running shoes. Four years in Australia and Spain. Four years of races in Germany, Switzerland, New Zealand, and around the world.

The first USA triathlete ever to win Olympic gold. She brought her hand to her mouth.

Gwen crossed the finish line, grabbed the tape and took four more steps. With heavy breaths, hands on her knees, she gripped the tape in her fists. She fumbled with it, straightened her posture and held it overhead while photographers clicked cameras. Her shoulders shook with sobs. Smiles appeared for photos, but between them, tears contorted her face. It was a weird combination of release, happiness, elation, joy and even disbelief. Where was Patrick? She thought hugging him would make it real. But everywhere were officials, reporters, barricades, fans.

I can't believe I did it, she thought. Gwen dropped the tape and put both hands to her face. Emotions rushed over her like a tide, waves of sensation pushing and pulling. Tears streamed. She walked in a circle, still looking for Patrick, and then bent over, crying, waiting for the rest of the athletes to finish. She felt her body exhale four years of stress and anticipation. She composed herself so she could congratulate each of her competitors who put so much into their own Olympic races.

Nicola Spirig's Thoughts

It was just some mental games—I knew she was a strong runner so I had to try everything to get her out of the rhythm a bit...I was very well prepared, and I haven't seen anyone running with her longer than I did today. I knew she was running really, really well, and I tried everything to beat her, but she was just too good in the moment.

Source: Shaw, Jené. "Inside the Jorgensen-Spirig Olympic Run Battle." *Triathlete. com*. August 20, 2016. Available: https://www.triathlete.com/events/inside-jorgensen-spirig-olympic-run-battle/.

History of Triathlon

In the 1970's, the San Diego Track Club invented triathlon as a training workout. In 1989, the International Triathlon Union (ITU) was formed in France and the first official World Championships were held there.

In 2013, in San Diego, California—the birthplace of triathlon—Gwen Jorgensen became the first American woman to win a World Triathlon Series race. In 2016, she became the first American triathlete to win Olympic gold.

In 2009, the Triathlon Mixed Relay was added to ITU racing. In this event, four athletes (female, male, female, male) each complete a super-sprint triathlon before tagging a teammate. In 2016, with Ben Kanute, Kirsten Kasper and Joe Maloy, Gwen was part of the World Champion Relay team. In her blog, Gwen said, "It was Team USA's first victory in the MTR and an absolute blast to compete in. It is short, fast and very difficult. It is a day I will never forget because of the pride I felt being a part of Team USA."

The first Olympic triathlon was at the Sydney 2000 Games. The Triathlon Mixed Relay became an Olympic event after the Rio 2016 Games. Olympic Triathlon Gold Medal Winners, Women:
    Sydney 2000—Brigitte McMahon (Switzerland)
    Athens 2004—Kate Allen (Austria)
    Beijing 2008—Emma Snowsill (Australia)
    London 2012—Nicola Spirig (Switzerland)
    Rio de Janeiro 2016—Gwen Jorgensen (USA)
    Tokyo 2020—Flora Duffy (Bermuda)

Olympic Gold Medal Winners, Men:
    Sydney 2000—Simon Whitfield (Canada)
    Athens 2004—Hamish Carter (New Zealand)
    Beijing 2008—Jan Frodeno (Germany)
    London 2012—Alistair Brownlee (Great Britain)
    Rio de Janeiro 2016—Alistair Brownlee (Great Britain)
    Tokyo 2020—Kristian Blummenfelt (Norway)

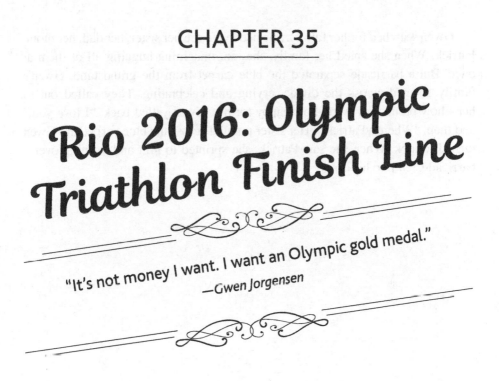

CHAPTER 35

Rio 2016: Olympic Triathlon Finish Line

"It's not money I want. I want an Olympic gold medal."
—Gwen Jorgensen

Gwen had no idea that after she passed Nicola, her lead increased. Forty seconds passed before Nicola crossed the finish line to win silver. When she did, Gwen welcomed her with a hug and tears.

Five seconds behind Nicola, two British athletes sprinted toward the finish. In the final meters, Vicky Holland edged out her compatriot by three seconds to win bronze.

Gwen congratulated them both with a hug and a pat on the back. Gwen's fellow Wollongong Wizard, Chilean Barbara Riveros, crossed the line in fifth. Gwen's USA teammate Katie Zaferes finished 18th. Sarah True, the third member of the women's USA team, sustained an injury and did not finish.

Gwen searched for her family. She needed to see her sister, her dad, her mom. Patrick. When she spied her family, she ran, imagining hugging all of them at once. But a barricade separated the blue carpet from the grandstand. Gwen's family shouted across the divide, crying and celebrating. They called out to her—how proud they were, how happy for her. Gwen yelled back, "I love you," and then, "Where's Patrick?" Her sister pointed across the blue carpet and Gwen turned to look. When she saw Patrick, she sprinted to him and, leaning over a barricade, fell into his arms.

CHAPTER 36

Rio 2016: Olympic Triathlon Medal Ceremony

> "There is power in what you tell yourself and for four years, I've said I aspire to win gold in Rio."
>
> —Gwen Jorgensen

After hugging Patrick, Gwen returned to the blue carpet and waited behind the awards podium. To her left, Vicky Holland of Great Britain. To her right, Nicola Spirig of Switzerland. In front, a three-tiered platform decorated with the Olympic rings and Rio 2016 logo. Behind, on the landscape, Sugarloaf Mountain. Gwen tried to memorize the moment.

Her sweaty hair pulled in a top bun, she wore a smile as strong as her tears. She looked down at her outfit, the USA Olympic champion uniform—a blue Nike-issued jacket with red and blue striped sleeves. On her chest, the United States Olympic Committee logo.

Vicky ascended the platform and received her medal. Nicola took the next higher step for hers. Then Gwen heard, "Gold Medalist and Olympic champion, representing the United States of America." An announcer repeated the words in Portuguese. Then, the English commentary continued: "Gwen Jorgensen."

Gwen stepped onto the platform's highest level. She raised both hands above her head. She waved to the crowd, to her family and friends in the grandstand. She looked behind the podium at Patrick and Jamie. She pointed, blew a kiss and said, "Thank you."

Then from a gold tray, an Olympic representative raised a multi-colored ribbon attached to a one-pound metal disk, 3.3 inches in diameter. Gwen bent forward. The representative slid the ribbon over Gwen's head. Gwen looked down. The gold medal.

She felt unusually emotional. Today represented four years of work and dedication. This was her investment actualized. Her goal achieved. Her potential realized.

She remembered watching the Olympics as a child and now, here she was. An Olympic champion. How many children were watching in their own homes? She hoped to instill the same pride in country that inspired her to follow a dream.

She brought herself back to the present. She shook Vicky's hand, then Nicola's, then turned to the American flag. Stress trickled away, along with years of build-up, anticipation and strain.

When the "Star-Spangled Banner" played, she laid her hand over her heart and sang.

Gwen's Olympic Gold Medal

Gwen with Olympic gold medal

At the first modern Olympic Games in 1896, the winner received a silver medal. Beginning in 1904, gold, silver and bronze medals were awarded to first, second and third place winners. The medals were attached to a ribbon with a pin for the winner's shirt. In 1960, the medals were designed to be worn around the athlete's neck. Many contemporary medals feature the goddess of victory and a representation of the host country's Olympic stadium.

The Rio 2016 gold medal design was regulated by the International Olympic Committee. It showed the Olympic emblem, the name of the Games, the name of the sport and the Organizing Committee of the Olympic Games' symbol.

CHAPTER 37

Rio 2016: Olympic Triathlon Media

"It was a mixture of emotions: joy, happiness, relief, pride, thankfulness, disbelief."

—Gwen Jorgensen

Immediately after the Olympic medal ceremony, the press approached. Television interviewers, radio commentators and print reporters.

Gwen told them how she felt. How she poured everything into this race. Tears frequently interrupted her story. She spoke about working every day, for four years, with this race in mind. She thanked her coach and her husband. She acknowledged her country and her teammates. She recognized the other women, all tough competitors.

Reporters at the triathlon site were the first of many. Gwen hadn't prepared for this part of the day, so she trusted her agent and sponsor representatives to take the lead. They would guide her through the next nine hours of photo sessions, interviews and media appearances.

First, a United States Olympic Committee representative whisked her to a press conference across the city at the International Broadcast Center (IBC). The IBC operated 24 hours a day and was based in two buildings set on the equivalent of seven soccer fields. There, she met with a group of reporters who were eager to secure quotes from the latest Olympic champion.

Then, she returned to Copacabana Beach and the NBC beachfront studio. Gwen climbed NBC's scaffolding to the green room. Her parents and uncles, Patrick's parents and sister Paige, and Elizabeth and Josh were there. Some friends had left to see various Olympic events, but others waited to congratulate her. She hugged them all. It was the first time she saw friends who had traveled 5,000 miles to watch her race. She never stopped smiling.

Gwen took off her medal so they could try it on. Adrenaline and excitement streamed through her; she wanted to share this feeling with the people who meant so much to her.

"Gwen, let's hurry, you need to get ready," the NBC producer said. In ten minutes, Gwen would appear live on television.

Gwen sat in a hairdresser's swivel chair. Her parents and friends took pictures, held the medal and monitored her name as it trended on social media. A woman worked on Gwen's head, still sweaty from competition.

"I'm so hungry," Gwen said. It was 3 p.m. and she hadn't eaten lunch. "I've only had a banana since the race."

Elizabeth offered her a plate. "Here. Someone brought you takeout. It's probably cold."

"I don't care. I'm starving. Can you cut it up and feed it to me while they do makeup?"

After Gwen's speed-styling, family and friends followed her and the producer out of the room and down the stairs to an open-air studio. Gwen joined an interviewer while her family and friends trailed a cameraman. Backstage, he shot video of them cheering and pumping their fists. It aired during Gwen's interview.

When the entourage returned to the green room, Gwen's agent said, "You have just a few minutes. Media at the IBC starts again soon. The car is waiting."

Gwen didn't know what to expect, but she didn't care. Her agent handled details and Pat was going with her. And she had the gold medal around her neck.

Elizabeth said, "What's the plan, Gwen?"

"I have no idea. You should go to the USA Triathlon party." Gwen started walking toward the car. "It starts at 5 and I'll be there at some point."

"At the USA House? We'll meet you."

***

While Gwen's family showered and dressed for the party, Gwen traveled to the IBC. The first thing she did was fill her plate at the athletes' buffet. With the nutrition she needed, she felt equipped for whatever came next.

At the interviews, she wore her podium jacket over a navy-blue USA t-shirt. On her face, a non-stop smile. "I'm just trying to really soak it all in, you know," she told a reporter. "It's been a long four years and a lot of blood, sweat and tears went into this."

Gwen went from one journalist to the next, talking about the race, about the medal ceremony, about her emotions. She mentioned her gratitude for Patrick and her coaching team. She said, "I was just thinking about all the investments [Jamie and Patrick] put into me, thinking about the four years, and it all came down to one day. To be able to actually execute on that day is pretty amazing."

Explaining the unusual conversation during the run, she said, "Nicola was really strong today on the bike and the run and...we were playing mind games," and, "Nicola and I were playing a bit of games, and neither of us wanted to lead in the headwind, so hopefully it made it exciting for the fans."

And then she spoke about her pride in triathlon and her country. "I'm just really super excited to win the first gold for triathlon for USA and hopefully it gets people into triathlon. It's a wonderful sport."

"I've said for four years that this was my goal," she told another reporter. "I wanted to cross that line and get the gold medal. It's pretty incredible that I was able to do it."

Gwen's Family Visited the Green Room

A green room is a space to gather before, during or after a show. The area is typically a small room with chairs, couches, water and snacks. It is a place to meet the producer or other guests, relax and check hair, makeup and appearance. The term may have come from a tradition to paint the walls of such a room green. This practice is no longer used, but the name remains.

Scenes from the green room

CHAPTER 38

Rio 2016: Olympic Triathlon Celebration

"Have a good support team around you."

—Gwen Jorgensen

While Gwen remained at the IBC giving interviews and posing for photos, Elizabeth texted her, describing the scene at the USA House. Team USA had renovated the seven-story school on Ipanema Beach, about two miles from Copacabana Beach. They improved the air conditioning, kitchens and Wi-Fi and decorated the exterior in red, white and blue lights. The way Elizabeth described it, Gwen could envision the shops for Olympic clothes, gifts and pins. The many rooms serving food. The top floor with 360-degree views of Rio.

Elizabeth told her the triathlon celebration was set up in a spacious room with wall-sized projection screens, high-top tables and benches. Waiters circulated with plates of food. On one giant screen, live athletics (track and field) played.

On another, the futebol (soccer) match. A third scrolled pictures of Gwen and the other USA triathletes: Sarah True, Katie Zaferes, Joe Maloy, Ben Kanute, Greg Billington. Photos from their childhood and college and professional days flashed on the screen.

Gwen felt like she was caught in a human tug of war. The International Broadcast Center, requesting photos and quotes, pulled in one direction. USA Triathlon, with their celebration at the USA House, yanked in the other. She checked her phone again. Elizabeth said USA teammate Sarah True praised Gwen for the win and typed in what Sarah said: *And what connects...is the sport of triathlon and the love we share for sport and competing...And at the end of the day, we are all winners because we are all Olympians.* Elizabeth said Gwen should hurry, that everyone was saying amazing things about her.

But she couldn't. The IBC required photos and interviews from all gold medal winners.

Finally, around 10 p.m., Gwen entered the USA House. From the party room, she heard guests chanting USA! USA! She walked in and when the crowd of 150 saw her, they shouted, clapped and whistled.

Andy Schmitz of USA Triathlon calmed the partygoers. He called Gwen to the front. She listened as he congratulated her and reviewed her rise from rookie triathlete to gold medal winner. Andy's speech reminded Gwen how far she'd come, how USA Triathlon found her, convinced her she had unexplored talent.

Claps and cheers interrupted him often. Then, he said, "Now, I'd like Gwen to take the mic and present the Order of Ikkos award." It was an honor each USA medal winner gave to one of their coaches.

Gwen stepped forward. The crowd cheered again. She tried to start her speech, but the ovation continued. She felt uncomfortable with the long applause.

"So, I'm not one to love getting up in front of crowds and giving speeches," she said. "But before I give this award out, I want to thank some other people who have really made this a success." She thanked Andy and USA Triathlon; her training partners; her coaches and support team; her family; her sponsors; and then, she looked at her husband. "And obviously Patrick has been a huge support member. He gave up his career to support me, and everyone who sees me or has been around me, has definitely seen Patrick as well. We know how hard he works, and I'd really like to give him a round of applause."

The crowd clapped and cheered for Patrick. Without him and all the others, Gwen knew she wouldn't have reached her potential.

"But for this award, I would like to give it to Jamie Turner."

Jamie came forward. Gwen opened the case, where his medallion rested on velvet. She presented it to him. They hugged, and the crowd applauded again.

Jamie gave a short speech and then everyone dispersed and mingled. Cameras flashed photos of the Olympians. Gwen talked to guests about the last few hours, the last few days and the last four years.

Gwen and Patrick had one more drink and snack and then hugged their family and friends. Gwen was exhausted but still wide awake. She didn't want the day to end.

Entrance to USA House

Gwen and Jamie at USA celebration

Rio 2016 USA Olympic triathlon team: Joe Maloy, Gwen, Ben Kanute, Greg Billington, Katie Zaferes, Sarah True

Gwen's Order of Ikkos Presentation

The Order of Ikkos is a medallion award recognizing the work of a coach or mentor. The award was established before the Beijing 2008 Olympic Games. The name comes from Ikkos of Tarentum who was the first Olympic coach in ancient Greece. In a ceremony at the USA House, each USA Olympic and Paralympic medalist honored a coach with this medal.

Gwen's Advice for Public Speaking

Although Gwen preferred talking to small groups, public speaking was part of her job: giving interviews, participating in press conferences, sitting on athlete panels and engaging in Q&A sessions. In addition to press responsibilities, her sponsors required motivational speeches to their employees or clients. Gwen even gave a convocation address at Carroll University in Waukesha, Wisconsin.

Gwen's tips for taking off the pressure:
- Prepare fully.
- Plan a clear message.
- Include slides to illustrate points.
- Practice in front of friends or family.
- Memorize themes, not words.
- Wear clothes that make you feel confident.
- Speak from the heart.
- Accept invitations to speak. Frequent practice leads to less stress.

CHAPTER 39

Rio 2016: The Day After the Olympic Triathlon

"I like to do things the hard way, I do not like to take a short cut...Hard work and dedication pay off."
—Gwen Jorgensen

The day after the Olympic race, Gwen, her family and friends arrived at the Oakley House for lunch. As one of her sponsors, the eyewear company hosted this celebration. Gwen and her guests sat at patio tables where sun filtered through a pergola. The ocean sent puffs of salty breeze across the lawn. Waiters filled champagne glasses. Gwen thought how lovely it was to have a place to celebrate in private with her favorite people. Patrick, her mom, dad, Elizabeth, Josh and her uncles. Friends from high school. Friends from college. To be able to share this unique, quiet celebration of a once-in-a-lifetime achievement. She didn't want to ever forget.

An Oakley representative spoke about Gwen's accomplishments, her grit on the Rio course, and said, "A toast." He raised his glass and everyone sipped. He presented gifts to Gwen and then directed the group to salads, meats, cakes, custards and ice cream. Gwen thought the food was impeccable, but the company even better.

After lunch and presentations, Gwen talked with Nicola Spirig (also an Oakley athlete). Although competitors on the course, they remained friends and colleagues.

"I admire you," Gwen said. "You are a mother and still train and compete at this level." Gwen and Patrick wanted to start their own family soon. Gwen thought about the female body, so strong and resilient. To give life and still perform physically.

***

At the end of the afternoon, Gwen found her own family. "So, Patrick and I aren't going to the Olympic Closing Ceremony," she said. "We booked flights for a New York media tour."

"Can we watch from home?" her mom said.

"I'll send links. Most are online." Gwen would spend a week promoting Team USA, the sport of triathlon and the Olympic Games. She planned to make notes on the plane, laying out her talking points. She would share her journey. The years of failing and succeeding. Of planning and re-evaluating. Of focusing not on the outcome but on the process. Of coaches, athletes, friends and family who became her teammates. Of years working every day. Of discovering and achieving her potential.

Gwen Admired Mother-Competitors at the Olympic Games

Women first competed in the Olympics at the Paris 1900 games. A mother and her daughter—Mary Perkins Ives Abbott and Margaret Abbott—participated in golf. Margaret won gold and her mother took seventh. Since the 1900 games, many American women competed at the Olympics, both before and after motherhood, including

- Sheryl Swoopes, basketball in Atlanta 1996, Sydney 2000 and Athens 2004;
- Joy Fawcett, soccer in Atlanta 1996, Sydney 2000 and Athens 2004;
- Dara Torres, swimming in Los Angeles 1984, Seoul 1988, Barcelona 1992 and Beijing 2008;
- Kerri Walsh Jennings, beach volleyball in Sydney 2000, Athens 2004, Beijing 2008, London 2012, and Rio de Janeiro 2016;
- Kristin Armstrong, cycling in Beijing 2008 and London 2012; and
- Kara Goucher, marathon in Beijing 2008 and London 2012.

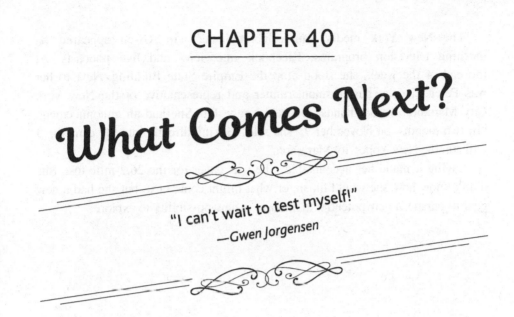

CHAPTER 40

What Comes Next?

"I can't wait to test myself!"
—*Gwen Jorgensen*

On the flight from Rio to New York, Gwen talked with Patrick about the future. She started as a swimmer, found strength as a runner and eventually tapped power as a triathlete. Although she could continue competing in triathlon, winning Olympic gold meant she reached her goal. She craved a new challenge. What else could she accomplish? Gwen couldn't stop thinking about what might be possible.

In the months leading up to the Olympics, she had talked to Patrick and Jamie. Could she compete with world-class runners? What if she didn't swim and bike before running? How fast could she go?

Running was her most powerful discipline and she wanted to explore it. She wanted to look, search and discover her potential.

***

The New York media tour celebrated her win. Gwen appeared on morning television programs, Facebook interviews and live podcasts. At the end of the week, she stood atop the Empire State Building. Next to her was Peter Ciaccia: businessman, runner and representative of the New York City Marathon. In her hands, she held a race bib. She had an announcement. "In two months, on November 7," she said, looking directly into the camera, "I will run the New York City Marathon."

Saying it made her accountable. She was eager for the 26.2-mile test. She didn't know how she would finish, or what might come next, but she had a new goal to pursue, a new potential to uncover, a new possibility to explore.

GWEN JORGENSEN
2016 Olympic Champion
Triathlon

Photo collage thank you gift for sponsors

A Letter from Gwen

Dear Reader,

I hope you enjoyed reading about triathlon and my Olympic dream. As you learn about your own potential, I recommend you focus on three things: core principles, recovery and gratitude. I hope they are helpful as you look, search and discover.

Practice Core Principles

- Surround yourself with talented, positive people.
- Announce your goals to hold yourself accountable.
- Journal achievements as well as areas to improve.
- Invest in yourself.
- Emphasize and capitalize on your strengths.
- Learn from your mistakes and correct weaknesses.
- Control the controllables.
- Get comfortable with the uncomfortable.
- Look ahead.
- Think positively.
- Be relentless in your pursuit.

Emphasize Recovery

In addition to fueling and training, I focus on recovering. Daily, I take a midday rest; if I can't sleep, I recline silently in bed for at least 30 minutes. Every night, I aim to be in bed by 8 p.m. Even if I'm not tired, I turn off electronics and lights and lay still. I use a sleep journal to recognize patterns and adjust my behaviors.

My recommendations for healthy sleep habits:
- Eat dinner early so it can digest before bed. If still hungry, have a snack of yogurt and granola or oatmeal.

- Create a bedtime routine.
- Go to bed at the same time every night.
- Remove television and phone from the bedroom.
- Set the room temperature to 61-67°.
- Use a white noise fan.
- Read or meditate.
- Make the room dark with blackout blinds or an eye mask.
- Keep a sleep journal to identify patterns.

Show Gratitude

I write thank you notes and give gifts to express appreciation. I know I can't reach my potential without the help of others, so each year, I recognize their support.

My recommendations for expressing gratitude:
- Handwrite letters, if possible.
- Start with a compliment.
- Be specific about what you are thankful for.
- Include a personalized or handmade touch.

Sincerely,
Gwen

Elizabeth

Thank you for so much! I don't even
know where to start... Thank you for coming
to Edmonton —it still seems surreal that you watched
me be crowned world champion. Although I wasn't able
to spend much time with you in Canada, I was so
happy you were there! Thank you for coming to the
Cities to dress shop. You were patient, kind, and selfless.
I had a great time and really valued your opinion.
Hope to see you again soon.
             Love,
                 gwen

Handwritten thank-you

BONUS CHAPTER

Setting Goals

Gwen achieved Olympic gold by setting two kinds of goals. First, she dreamed of being the Olympic Champion. This was her outcome goal.

Gwen imagined Olympic gold, but knew she couldn't guarantee that outcome. So, she set specific daily process goals to help achieve her dream. These were the tasks she focused on. For example, in swimming keep her elbows high. For running, relax her shoulders. For biking, practice mounts and dismounts.

As she set process goals, she asked her mentors questions.

1. Is this a realistic goal?
2. Do you have suggestions for other goals?
3. Where can I focus to improve my performance?

4. What can I do to increase my enjoyment?
5. What can I do to further my learning?

In forming her outcome and process goals, Gwen recommends these actions:

- Write down outcome and process goals.
  - » Settle on a few specific, achievable goals.
- Discuss goals with trusted adults.
  - » Mentors could include coaches, teachers, parents, private teachers, friends or therapists.
  - » Routinely discuss and evaluate progress with mentors.
- Document progress daily.
  - » Build tools into routine, like journaling and daily reflection.
- Revise goals as needed.

Example Process and Outcome Goals

Although Gwen's goals were athletic, goals can be applied to any dream.

A writer might aspire to publish a novel, and their process goals could be to

- read admired authors
- attend a writing workshop
- write five hundred words every day
- at the end of every workshop, edit unnecessary words

A pianist might want to solo with an orchestra, but their process goals could be to

- listen to professional recordings
- warm up with scales to begin each practice
- every day, work all parts of a piece, not just the first page
- be conscious of curving the fingers and keeping forearms level

Accountability

Gwen used a daily journal to keep herself accountable. Every day, she noted three successes and three things to improve. Other tools could include a daily checklist, check-ins with a coach, or meeting teammates for practices, meal-planning or recovery.

Improvement happens slowly, one day at a time. It is important to show up for every practice and focus on specific process goals. But know that progress isn't linear. There will be days when things don't go well. That's okay. Just try again the next day.

Advice from Gwen: Strive for what is sustainable—what is the best effort you can maintain daily? Focus on finding your best average instead of excelling every day. Remember, there is value in rest days and time away from your goals.

Daily

List three things you've done well and three things to improve.

Monthly

Summarize your accomplishments and improvements. This will build confidence.

Questions Gwen Recommends

Before you commit to an outcome or process goal, answer the following questions:

- What are your dreams?
- What are your values? What do you stand for and how does that fit with your goals?
- What physiological, tactical, and technical areas do you want to improve?
- What has worked in the past? What hasn't worked?
- What do you want from mentors? What support system do you need?
- What will you do to help others? How will your goals benefit others?
- What are you prepared to do to achieve your dreams?

Advice from Gwen: When filling out the **Goal Setting Worksheet**, don't worry if some lines are blank. Do what works best for you and your goals. Ask mentors for guidance or assistance.

GOAL SETTING WORKSHEET

Outcome goals (big ambitions)

1. _____

2. _____

Process goals (specific, daily tasks to help achieve your ambitions)

1. _____

2. _____

3. _____

4. _____

5. _____

Mentors

1. _____

2. _____

3. _____

4. _____

5. _____

Questions or topics to discuss with mentors

1. _____

2. _____

3. _____

4. _____

5. _____

Methods to track progress

1. _____

2. _____

3. _____

4. _____

5. _____

Dear Reader

Thank you for reading. You can learn more about me at gwenjorgensen.com and Youtube.com/gwenJorgensen

Stay active and enjoy your journey!

Love,

Gwen

PS Message me on social media @gwenJorgensen

Acknowledgments

Our biggest thank you to Gwen. Your letters to the reader and personal artifacts make this book come to life. Your story is one of inspiration and dedication. Thank you for being you, for putting in the work, and for sharing your process with us.

Thank you to those who helped Gwen achieve her dreams: Dave Anderson, Cindi Bannink, Blaine Carlson, Craig and Larry Lanza, Eric Lehmann, Patrick Lemieux, Barb Lindquist, Bobby McGee, Andy Schmitz, Tom Schuler, Jim Stintzi, Jamie Turner, Team USA, USA Triathlon. Thank you also to the countless others who were integral to the journey—fans, training partners, teammates, sponsors.

We are also thankful to the group of highly talented people who worked with us. Thank you Kathie Giorgio, Allwriters' Workplace & Workshop, and the Tuesday night book writers group. Thank you, Liza Wiemer for suggestions and edits. Thank you, beta reader, Emily Reddy.

Thank you to all who offered pre-publication support and endorsements: Flora Duffy, Taylor Knibb, Barb Lindquist, Alexi Pappas, Liza Wiemer, Katie Zaferes.

Thank you to Joel Jorgensen and Josh Olson for always supporting us.

Thank you, Liz Evans and Meyer & Meyer Sport, for believing in the project and story, and for giving our voice a home.

This memoir is for you, young reader, so thank you for reading. We hope you are inspired to follow your own dreams.

Nancy, Gwen, and Elizabeth Jorgensen

Credits

Cover design: Annika Naas
Interior design: Anja Elsen
Layout: DiTech Publishing Services, www.ditechpubs.com
Cover photo: picture alliance / dpa | Barbara Walton
Interior photos: All photos courtesy of the authors unless otherwise noted; chapter 16: p. 72 Courtesy of Talbot Cox; chapter 25: p. 108 Courtesy of Johnathan Pavlica
Managing editor: Elizabeth Evans
Copy editing: Stephanie Kramer